Practical Handbook of

Dewey Decimal Classification

Practical Handbook of
Dewey Decimal Classification

Dr. C.K. Sharma

ATLANTIC®

PUBLISHERS & DISTRIBUTORS

Published by

ATLANTIC

PUBLISHERS & DISTRIBUTORS (P) LTD

B-2, Vishal Enclave, Opp. Rajouri Garden,
New Delhi-110027
Phones : +91-11-25413460, 25429987, 25466842

Sales Office
7/22, Ansari Road, Darya Ganj,
New Delhi-110002
Phones : +91-11-23273880, 23275880, 23280451
Fax : +91-11-23285873
web : www.atlanticbooks.com
e-mail : info@atlanticbooks.com

Branch Office
5, Nallathambi Street, Wallajah Road,
Chennai-600002
Phones : +91-44-64611085, 32413319
e-mail : chennai@atlanticbooks.com

Printed in India
at Nice Printing Press, Delhi

Preface

It is my privilege to present one more book in the field of library science. The importance of Dewey Decimal Classification (DDC), which is world's most widely used library classification system, remains the same as it was at the time of its evolution in 1876. Even in computerisation of a library, classification is very much helpful. DDC is a method of classifying and cataloguing library materials by subject. It is the simplest scheme of coordinating the titles on the same subject and on related subjects by using a combination of letters and numbers so as to make items easier to locate on the shelves of the library. Though DDC has no scientific base and does not follow scientific principles, it is enumerated and can be easily understood. This scheme is applied in almost all the Indian libraries and as such it is gainful for all to have acquaintance with this system.

The Dewey System attempts to organise all knowledge into ten main classes:

- 000 Generalities
- 500 Natural Science and Mathematics
- 100 Philosophy and Psychology
- 600 Technology (Applied Sciences)
- 200 Religion
- 700 Arts
- 300 Social Science
- 800 Literature
- 400 Language
- 900 Geography and History

I have tried to learn DDC and submit a sketch of this scheme of classification which will help the students and teachers to practice it.

I am grateful to the authors of many books on classifications whose books I studied and consulted. My thanks are due to my friends and students who always cooperate with me in my academic work.

I am also thankful to the Chairman, M/s Atlantic Publishers and Distributors, New Delhi who has taken keen interest in the field of Library Science.

C.K. SHARMA

Contents

1

Introduction

MELVILLE LOUIS KOSSUTH DEWEY
(Dec. 10, 1851 – Dec. 26, 1931)

Father & Mother – Joel and Eliza Dewey

Born   – Dec. 10, 1851 at Adam Centre, New York

His father was shoemaker and run a general store.

The family was not well to do.

During childhood Melvil Dewey did odd jobs and helped his father in his store. His education discontinued.

His education was restarted. At the age of 17 he became a teacher on a meager salary; seven years later (at the age of 24) in 1870 he entered Amherst College, Massachusetts. He graduated in 1874.

While he was a student he became an Asstt. Librarian of College Library.

- He was economical and hard working.
- At Amherst College he learned shorthand and enlisted in the campaign for reformed spelling.
- He was given the work of classifying books with his own method to find the fixed location of the books.
- He soon sought a device, a method to meet the growing number of subjects.
- He made personal visit to many libraries and consulted experts and discussed library problems.

- He was confident of getting a solution of problems.
- He used Indo-Arabic numerals while reforming the spellings.
- He used decimal fractions to denote the contents of the books within a classified system.
- He had deep affection with Indo-Arabic numerals.
- On May 8, 1873 he presented a plan to organize the collection of the library, before the library committee.
- His plan was accepted by the committee.
- In April 1876, Dewey left Amherst College and went to Boston and founded American Library Journal with Fredrick Leypoldt and R.R. Walker and edited until 1880.
- He helped in organizing a <u>conference</u> of librarians at Philadelphia on Oct. 4-6, 1876.
- This conference gave birth to American Library Association. Dewey was Secretary of the Association from 1876 to 1890, and President in 1890-91 and 1892-93.
- He also created the "Library Bureau" to supply library stationery and labour saving equipments and remained President for 25 years.
- He was President of American Metric Bureau.
- On Oct. 9, 1876, Dewey married Annie R. Godfrey, the Librarian of Wellesley College.
- In 1883, Dewey moved to Columbia College (Now Columbia University) on a salary of $3500 per year.
- He founded co-educational library school in Jan. 1, 1887.
- During his stay at Columbia two more editions of DDC appeared under the editorship of Walter Stanley Biscal (1853-1933).
- He resigned on Dec. 20, 1888 from Columbia College.
- He became Secretary of Board of Regents of the University of State of New York and Director of New York State Library.

- In 1889, Dewey resigned from Secretaryship.
- In 1892, he founded New York Lib. Association.
- In Jan. 1, 1906, he resigned from the State Library.
- He continued his association with librarianship until the end of his life.
- In 1922, Dewey moved to Mirror Lake, New York.
- In 1927 the editorial office of DDC moved to Library of Congress in Washington.
- The Publishing responsibility was taken by Forest Press.
- 12th edition (1927) was the last came under the Dewey's scrutiny.
- In August 1922, Annie Godfrey Dewey died.
- In May 1924, Dewey married a family friend Mrs. Emily Mckay Beal.

Dewey died of a stroke on <u>Dec. 26, 1931,</u> when the 13th edition was in the making.

Dewey Decimal Classification (DDC)

When Dewey was Asstt. Librarian of Amherst College, he created a solution to classify the college collection <u>in 1873.</u>

<u>Dewey said</u> "For months I dreamed night and day that there must be some solution. In future, there will be thousands of libraries having millions of collection. The solution should be the simplest system. One Sunday, during the long sermon by St. Sterns, while I looked on his face without hearing a word, the solution flashed over me. I jumped in my seat and came out near shouting 'Eureka'. It was to get absolute simplicity by using the simplest known symbols, the Arabic numerals as decimals, with the ordinary significance of <u>nought</u> (zero), to number a classification of all human knowledge in print; this supplemented by the next simplest known symbols a, b, c, indexing all heds of the table so that it would be easier to use a classification with 1000 heds so keyed than to use the ordinary 30 or 40 heds which one had to study carefully before using.*"

---

* While Dewey was alive he personally oversaw editorial production and controlled money matters.

The scheme was first applied in Amherst College and printed classification was produced through the efforts of W.S. Biscoe, the faculty of Amherst. DDC was published anonymously in 1876 under the title "A Classification and Subject Index for cataloguing and arranging books and pamphlets of a library." Dewey delivered 150 copies to Amherst. The booklet consisted of 44 pages including introduction and the Index.

DDC was discussed again at the conference of librarians held in London in 1877.

2nd Edition — entitled *Decimal Classification and Relative Index* appeared in 1885. Biscoe, W.S. followed Dewey in Columbia College, assisted in its development. This edition was copyrighted by Library Bureau, a Library Supplier Co. founded by Dewey.

Editions	Pages	Copies	Editor
1. 1876	44	1000	Melvil Dewey
2. 1885	314	500	Melvil Dewey and W.S. Biscoe
3. 1888	416	500	Melvil Dewey and W.S. Biscoe
4. 1891	466	1000	May Seymour
5. 1894	467	2000	May Seymour
6. 1899	511	7600	May Seymour
7. 1911	792	2000	May Seymour
8. 1913	850	2000	May Seymour
9. 1915	856	3000	May Seymour
10. 1919	940	4000	May Seymour
11. 1922	944	5000	Dorkas Fellows
12. 1927	1243	9340	Dorkas Fellows
13. 1932	1647	9750	Dorkas Fellows & M.W. Getchell
14. 1942	1927	15632	Constantin Mazney & " "
15. 1951	716	11200	Milton J. Fergson
16. 1958	2439	31011	Benjamin A. Cluster & D. Haykin
17. 1965	2153	38677	Benjamin A. Cluster & D. Haykin
Rev.17 1967	2480	(Total pages)	Benjamin A. Cluster & D. Haykin
INDEX			
18. 1971	2718	–	Benjamin A. Cluster & D. Haykin
19. 1979	3361	–	Benjamin A. Cluster & D. Haykin
20. 1989			Benjamin A. Cluster & D. Haykin

Abridged Edition

The Dewey Decimal Classification first Edition of 1876 containing 1000 three figure class number was criticized as being overly detailed. This initial criticism attested to Dewey's sense and vision of the future.

- In 1894, an outline of the scheme was issued in addition to a regular full edition.
- At first, the new edition of abridged edition was issued independently.
- It was published later as and when needed.
- 6th abridged edition was directly abridged from the 14th unabridged edition.
- This policy continued upto 9th abridged edition.
- The 10th edition was not strictly abridged version of 10th edition (1971). It was an adaptation of the letter of a few points. This was criticized.
- The old policy was reinstated.
- 12th abridged edition was issued in Jan. 1989.

The Abridged edition has following special features:

- It can be used upto 20000 documents in a library.
- It is abridged in terms of expansion of subjects.
- Main classes are assigned notation 0 to 9 from .0000001 to .9999999.
- 0 is nothing but 1 is universe.

MAIN CLASSES

Dewey divided the universe of knowledge in 10 Divisions. Each division represents one discipline of subject/knowledge. 10 divisions are categorised as under:

0.0   Generalia
0.1   Philosophy and related discipline
0.2   Religion
0.3   Social Sciences
0.4   Languages
0.5   Pure Science

0.6   Technology (Applied Science)

0.7   The Arts

0.8   Literature (Belles-Science)

0.9   Gen. Geography and his being and their auxiliaries.

HOW TO CONSULT SCHEDULE

1. Direct approach through schedule:

    (a) Find out the <u>subject matter</u> of the book.

    (b) Find out the <u>point of view</u> in which subject has been treated.

    (c) Find out in what <u>form the subject is presented</u> in book.

    (d) Choose the main class on the basis of (a), (b), (c).

    (e) Choose the first sub-division of 100 (second summary).

    (f) Choose the third summary.

    (g) Look at the schedules.

2. Indirect approach through the index:

    (a) Select a key word which will represent our subject.

    (b) Enter the Index through the selected key word.

    (c) Go to the schedules and confirm the number.

Difficult Cases

1. Books of fanciful title: Push and Pull, small is beautiful.

2. Book on subjects on which class number is not possible, example: Classification of Public library — To classify under classification.

3. New subjects for which class No. not provided: put under broader subject.

4. Book dealing with two or more subjects equally treated: classify with broader subject.

DDC was first used in —

1. **Great Britain** : In Oct. 1877 at the time of Historical Conference of Librarians in London. The LA (GB) was founded in this conference also.

More than 50% libraries adopted this scheme by 1910.

2. It was first used in India in 1915 by a famous American Librarian and writer Asa Don Dickinson (1876-1960), a student of Dewey. It was first adopted by Imperial Library, Calcutta. Now it is used in more than 80% libraries in India.

3. On 80th birthday (1931) Melvil Dewey claimed that DDC is used in 20 nations and also in National Library of India (Oct. 1964).

4. Many bibliographical services, trade bibliographies and centralized cataloguing agencies and MARC programme used the system to organize their bibliographical wares. DDC was also used by Booklist (ALA). Publishers weekly (R.R. Warker), American Book Publishing Record (R.R. Warker), Book Review digest, British Book News (British Council), Indian Books in print, Sears list of subject headings (Broader numbers). In (1958) Australian Nation Bibliography, Sri Lankan National Bibliography, and Canadiana (Canada National Bibliography) used DDC.

DDC authorities restoring the following methods to make it equally useful to varied users of different cultures and nations —

1. Expansion of Non-American subjects
2. Sponsoring International Survey and Seminars
3. For official translations
4. Involvement of experts from difficult cultures in preparing and revising schedules.

Hindi versions based on DDC

1. Dewey (1976) — P.N. Gaur translated DC in Hindi which is not appropriate and uptodate.

2. DDC adopted technique for Hindi literature used —

   8 H0 – Base No. for Hindi literature filed before 810

   4 H0 – Base No. for Hindi language instead of 491.43

   4 H5 – instead of 491.435 for Hindi Grammar.

SECOND SUMMARY
The 100 Divisions*

000	**Generalities**
010	Bibliography
020	Library & information sciences
030	General encyclopedic works
040	
050	General serial publications
060	General organizations & museology
070	Journalism, publishing, newspapers
080	General collections
090	Manuscripts & book rarities
100	**Philosophy & related disciplines**
110	Metaphysics
120	Epistemology, causation, humankind
130	Paranormal phenomena & arts
140	Specific philosophical viewpoints
150	Psychology
160	Logic
170	Ethics (Moral philosophy)
180	Ancient, Medieval, Oriental
190	Modern Western philosophy
200	**Religion**
210	Natural religion
220	Bible
230	Christian theology
240	Christian moral & devotional
250	Local church & religious orders
260	Social & ecclesiastical theology
270	History & geography of church
280	Christian denominations & sects
290	Other & comparative religions
300	**Social Sciences**
310	Statistics
320	Political science
330	Economics
340	Law
350	Public administration

360	Social problems & services
370	Education
380	Commerce (Trade)
390	Customs, etiquette, folklore
400	**Language**
410	Linguistics
420	English & Anglo-Saxon languages
430	Germanic languages German
440	Romance languages French
450	Italian, Romanian, Rhaeto-Romanic
460	Spanish & Portuguese languages
470	Italic languages Latin
480	Hellenic Classical Greek
490	Other languages
500	**Pure Sciences**
510	Mathematics
520	Astronomy & allied sciences
530	Physics
540	Chemistry & allied sciences
550	Sciences of earth & other worlds
560	Paleontology
570	Life sciences
580	Botanical sciences
590	Zoological sciences
600	**Technology (Applied Sciences)**
610	Medical sciences
620	Engineering & allied operations
630	Agriculture & related technologies
640	Home economics & family living
650	Management & auxiliary services
660	Chemical & related technologies
670	Manufactures
680	Manufacture for specific uses
690	Buildings
700	**The Arts**
710	Civic & landscape art
720	Architecture
730	Plastic arts Sculpture

740	Drawing, decorative & minor arts
750	Painting & paintings
760	Graphic Arts Prints
770	Photography & photographs
780	Music
790	Recreational & performing arts
800	**Literature (Belles-letters)**
810	American Literature in English
820	English & Anglo-Saxon literatures
830	Literatures of Germanic languages
840	Literature of Romance languages
850	Italian, Romanian, Rhaeto-Romanic
860	Spanish & Portuguese literatures
870	Italic literatures Latin
880	Hellenic literatures Greek
890	Literatures of other languages
900	**General geography & history**
910	General geography Travel
920	General biography & genealogy
930	General history of Ancient world
940	General history of Europe
950	General history of Asia
960	General history of Africa
970	General history of North America
980	General history of South America
990	General history of other areas

* Consult schedules for complete and exact headings

THIRD SUMMARY
000 Generalities*

000	**Generalities**
001	Knowledge
002	The book
003	Systems
004	
005	
006	
007	

INTRODUCTION 11

008
009
010 **Bibliography**
011 Bibliographies
012 Of individuals
013 Of works by specific classes of writers
014 Of anonymous & pseudonymous work
015 Of works from specific places
016 Subject bibliographies & catalogues
017 General subject catalogues
018 Author & date catalogues
019 Dictionary catalogues
020 **Library & Information Sciences**
021 Library relationships
022 Physical plant
023 Personnel & positions
024
025 Library operations
026 Libraries for specific subjects
027 General libraries
028 Reading and use of information media
029
030 **General encyclopedic works**
031 American
032 Others in English
033 In other Germanic languages
034 In French, Provençal, Catalan
035 In Italian, Romanian, Rhaeto-Romanic
036 In Spanish & Portuguese
037 In Slavic languages
038 In Scandinavian languages
039 In other languages
040
041
042
043
044
045

046
047
048
049
050 **General serial publications**
051 American
052 Others in English
053 In other Germanic languages
054 In French, Provençal, Catalan
055 In Italian, Romanian, Rhaeto-Romanic
056 In Spanish & Portuguese
057 In Slavic languages
058 In Scandinavian languages
059 In other languages
060 **General organizations & museology**
061 In North America
062 In British Isles
063 In Central Europe
064 In France & Monaco
065 In Italy & adjacent territories
066 In Iberian Peninsula & adjacent islands
067 In Eastern Europe
068 In other areas
069 Museology (Museum Science)
070 **Journalism, publishing, newspapers**
071 In North America
072 In British Isles
073 In Central Europe
074 In France & Monaco
075 In Italy & adjacent islands
076 In Iberian Peninsula & adjacent islands
077 In Eastern Europe
078 In Scandinavia
079 In other areas
080 **General collections**
081 American
082 Others in English
083 In other Germanic languages

084 In French, Provençal, Catalan
085 In Italian, Romanian, Rhaeto-Romanic
086 In Spanish & Portuguese
087 In Slavic languages
088 In Scandinavian languages
089 In other languages
090 **Manuscripts & book rarities**
091 Manuscripts
092 Block books
093 Incunabula
094 Printed books
095 Books notable for bindings
096 Notable illustrations & materials
097 Notable ownership or origin
098 Works notable for content
099 Books notable for format

    * Consult schedules for complete and exact headings.

100 PHILOSOPHY AND RELATED DISCIPLINES
100 **Philosophy and related disciplines**
101 Theory of philosophy
102 Miscellany of philosophy
103 Dictionaries of philosophy
104
105 Serials on philosophy
106 Organizations of philosophy
107 Study & teaching of philosophy
108 Treatment among groups of persons
109 Historical treatment of philosophy
110 **Metaphysics**
111 Ontology
112
113 Cosmology
114 Space
115 Time
116 Evolution
117 Structure
118 Force & energy
119 Number & quantity

120 **Epistemology, causation, humankind**
121 Epistemology
122 Causation
123 Determinism & indeterminism
124 Teleology
125
126 The self
127 The unconscious and the subconscious
128 Humankind
129 Origin and destiny of individual souls
130 **Paranormal phenomena & arts**
131 Well-being, happiness, success
132
133 Parapsychology & occultism
134
135 Dreams & mysteries
136
137 Analytic & divinatory graphology
138 Physiognomy
139 Phrenology
140 **Specific philosophical viewpoints**
141 Idealism and related systems and doctrines
142 Critical philosophy
143 Intuitionism & Bergsonism
144 Humanism and related systems
145 Sensationalism & ideology
146 Naturalism and related systems
147 Pantheism and related systems
148 Liberalism and other systems
149 Other systems and doctrines
150 **Psychology**
151
152 Physiological psychology
153 Intelligence & intellect
154 Subconscious states and processes
155 Differential and genetic psychology
156 Comparative psychology
157 Abnormal & clinical psychologies

196 Spain & Portugal
197 Russia & Finland
198 Scandinavia
199 Other geographical areas

200 RELIGION

200 **Religion**
201 Philosophy of Christianity
202 Miscellany of Christianity
203 Dictionaries of Christianity
204 Special topics of general applicability
205 Serials on Christianity
206 Organizations of Christianity
207 Study & teaching of Christianity
208 Christianity among groups of persons
209 History & geography of Christianity
210 **Natural religion**
211 Concepts of God
212 Nature of God
213 Creation
214 Theodicy
215 Science & religion
216 Good & evil
217
218 Humankind
219 Analogy
220 **Bible**
221 Old Testament
222 Historical books of Old Testament
223 Poetic books of Old Testament
224 New Testament
225 New Testament
226 Gospels & Acts
227 Epistles
228 Revelation (Apocalypse)
229 Apocrypha & pseudopigrapha
230 **Christian theology**
231 God
232 Jesus Christ & his family

233 Humankind
234 Salvation (Soteriology) & grace
235 Spiritual beings
236 Eschatology
237
238 Creeds & confessions of faith
239 Apologetics & polemics
240 Christian moral & devotional theology
241 Moral theology
242 Devotional literature
243 Evangelistic writings for individuals
244
245 Hymns without music
246 Art in Christianity
247 Church furnishings & articles
248 Christian experience, practice, life
249 Christian observances in family life
250 Local church & religious orders
251 Preaching (Homiletics)
252 Texts of sermons
253 Secular clergymen and duties
254 Parish government & administration
255 Religion congregations and orders
256
257
258
259 Parochial activities
260 Social & ecclesiastical theology
261 Social theology
262 Ecclesiology
263 Times & places of religious observance
264 Public worship
265 Other rites, ceremonies, ordinances
266 Missions
267 Associations for religious work
268 Religious training & instruction
269 Spiritual renewal
270 History & geography of church

271   Religious congregations and orders
272   Persecutions
273   Doctrinal controversies and heresies
274   Christian Church in Europe
275   Christian Church in Asia
276   Christian Church in Africa
277   Christian Church in North America
278   Christian Church in South America
279   Christian Church in other areas
280   Christian denominations & sects
281   Primitive & Oriental churches
282   Roman Catholic Church
283   Anglican churches
284   Protestants of Continental origin
285   Presbyterian and related churches
286   Baptist, Disciples, Adventist
287   Methodist churches
288   Unitarianism
289   Other denominations and sects
290   Other comparative religions
291   Comparative religion
292   Classical (Greek & Roman) religion
293   Germanic religion
294   Religions of Indic origin
295   Zoroastrianism
296   Judaism
297   Islam & religions derived from it
298
299   Other religions

300 SOCIAL SCIENCES

300   Social sciences
301   Sociology
302   Social interaction
303   Social processes
304   Relation of natural factors
305   Social stratification
306   Culture and institutions

307 Communities
308
309
310 Statistics
311
312 Statistics of populations
313
314 General statistics of Europe
315 General statistics of Asia
316 General statistics of Africa
317 General statistics of North America
318 General statistics of South America
319 General statistics of other areas
320 Political Science
321 Kinds of governments and states
322 Relation of state to social groups
323 Relation of state to its residents
324 The political process
325 International migration
326 Slavery & emancipation
327 International relations
328 Legislation
329
330 Economics
331 Labor economics
332 Financial economics
333 Land economics
334 Cooperatives
335 Socialism and related systems
336 Public finance
337 International economies
338 Production
339 Macroeconomies and related topics
340 Law
341 International law
342 Constitutional & administrative law
343 Miscellaneous public law
344 Social law

345 Criminal law
346 Private law
347 Civil procedure & courts
348 Statutes, regulations, cases
349 Law of individual states & nations
350 Public Administration
351 Central governments
352 Local governments
353 U.S. federal & state governments
354 Other central governments
355 Military art & science
356 Foot forces & warfare
357 Mounted forces & warfare
358 Armoured, technical, air, space forces
359 Sea (Naval) forces & warfare
360 Social problems & services
361 Social problems & welfare
362 Social welfare problems & services
363 Other social problems & services
364 Criminology
365 Penal institutions
366 Association
367 General clubs
368 Insurance
369 Miscellaneous kinds of associations
370 Education
371 Generalities of education
372 Elementary education
373 Secondary education
374 Adult education
375 Curriculums
376 Education of women
377 Schools & religion
378 Higher education
379 Education and the state
380 Commerce (Trade)
381 Internal commerce
382 International commerce

383 Postal communication
384 Other systems of communication
385 Railroad transportation
386 Inland waterway & ferry transportation
387 Water, air, space transportation
388 Ground transportation
389 Metrology & standardization
390 Customs, etiquette, folklore
391 Costume & personal appearance
392 Customs of life cycle & domestic life
393 Death customs
394 General customs
395 Etiquette (Manners)
396
397
398 Folklore
399 Customs of war & diplomacy

400 LANGUAGE

400 Language
401 Philosophy of theory
402 Miscellany
403 Dictionaries & encyclopedias
404 Special topics of general applicability
405 Serial publications
406 Organizations
407 Study & teaching
408 Treatment among groups of persons
409 Historical & geographical treatment
410 Linguistics
411 Notations
412 Etymology
413 Polyglot dictionaries
414 Phonology
415 Structural systems (Grammar)
416
417 Dialectology & paleography
418 Usage (Applied linguistics)

419   Verbal language not spoken or written
420   English & Anglo-Saxon languages
421   Written & spoken English
422   English etymology
423   English dictionaries
424
425   English structural system
426
427   Nonstandard English
428   Standard English usage
429   Anglo-Saxon (Old English)
430   Germanic languages — German
431   Written & spoken German
432   German etymology
433   German dictionaries
434
435   German structural system
436
437   Nonstandard German
438   Standard German usage
439   Other Germanic languages
440   Romance languages — French
441   Written & spoken French
442   French etymology
443   French dictionaries
444
445   French structural system
446
447   Nonstandard French
448   Standard French usage
449   Provençal & Catalan
450   Italian, Romanian, Rhaeto-Romanic
451   Written & spoken Italian
452   Italian etymology
453   Italian dictionaries
454
455   Italian structural system
456

500 PURE SCIENCES

500 **Pure sciences**
501 Philosophy & theory
502 Miscellany
503 Dictionaries & encyclopedias
504
505 Serial publications
506 Organizations
507 Study & teaching
508 Travel & surveys
509 Historical & geographical treatment
510 **Mathematics**
511 Generalities
512 Algebra
513 Arithmetic
514 Topology
515 Analysis
516 Geometry
517
518
519 Probabilities & applied mathematics
520 **Astronomy & allied sciences**
521 Theoretical astronomy
522 Practical & spherical astronomy
523 Descriptive astronomy
524
525 Earth (Astronomical geography)
526 Mathematical geography
527 Celestial navigation
528 Ephemerides (Nautical almanacs)
529 Chronology (Time)
530 **Physics**
531 Mechanics
532 Mechanics of fluids
533 Mechanics of gases
534 Sound and related vibrations
535 Light and paraphotic phenomena
536 Heat

537 Electricity & electronics
538 Magnetism
539 Modern Physics
540 Chemistry & allied sciences
541 Physical & theoretical chemistry
542 Laboratories, apparatus, equipment
543 Analytical chemistry
544 Qualitative chemistry
545 Quantitative chemistry
546 Inorganic chemistry
547 Organic chemistry
548 Crystallography
549 Mineralogy
550 Sciences of Earth & other worlds
551 Geology, meteorology, hydrology
552 Petrology (Rocks)
553 Economic geology
554 Treatment in Europe
555 Treatment in Asia
556 Treatment in Africa
557 Treatment in North America
558 Treatment in South America
559 Treatment in other areas and worlds
560 Paleontology
561 Paleobotany
562 Fossil invertebrates
563 Fossil Protozoa and other simple animals
564 Fossil Mollusca & molluscoidea
565 Other fossil invertebrates
566 Fossil Chordata
567 Fossil cold-blooded vertebrates
568 Fossil Aves (Fossil birds)
569 Fossil Mammalia
570 Life Sciences
571   .
572 Human races
573 Physical anthropology
574 Biology

575 Organic evolution & genetics
576 Microbes
577 General nature of life
578 Microscopy in biology
579 Collection and preservation of specimens
580 **Botanical Sciences**
581 Botany
582 Spematophyta
583 Dicotyledones
584 Monocotyledones
585 Gymnospermae
586 Cryptogamia
587 Pteridophyta
588 Bryophyta
589 Thallophyta
590 **Zoological Sciences**
591 Zoology
592 Invertebrates
593 Protozoa and other simple animals
594 Mollusca & molluscoidea
595 Other invertebrates
596 Chordata
597 Cold-blooded vertebrates
598 Aves (Birds)
599 Mammalia (Mammals)

600 TECHNOLOGY (APPLIED SCIENCES)

600 **Technology (Applied sciences)**
601 Philosophy & theory
602 Miscellany
603 Dictionaries & encyclopedias
604 General technologies
605 Serial publications
606 Organizations & management
607 Study & teaching
608 Inventions & patents
609 Historical & geographical treatment
610 **Medical Sciences — Medicine**

611 Human anatomy, cytology, tissues
612 Human physiology
613 General & personal hygiene
614 Public health and related topics
615 Pharmacology & therapeutics
616 Diseases
617 Surgery and related topics
618 Other branches of medicine
619 Experimental medicine
620 **Engineering and allied operations**
621 Applied physics
622 Mining and related operations
623 Military & nautical engineering
624 Civil engineering
625 Railroads, roads, highways
626
627 Hydraulic engineering
628 Sanitary & municipal engineering
629 Other branches of engineering
630 **Agriculture and related technologies**
631 Crops and their production
632 Pant injuries, diseases, pests
633 Field crops
634 Orchards, fruits, forestry
635 Garden crops — Vegetables
636 Animal husbandry
637 Dairy and related technologies
638 Insect culture
639 Nondomestic animals & plants
640 **Home Economics & family living**
641 Food & drink
642 Meal and table service
643 Housing & household equipment
644 Household utilities
645 Furnishing and decorating home
646 Sewing, clothing, personal living
647 Public households
648 Housekeeping

649   Child rearing & care of sick
650   **Management and auxiliary services**
651   Office services
652   Written communication processes
653   Shorthand
654
655
656
657   Accounting
658   General management
659   Advertising & public relations
660   **Chemical & related technologies**
661   Industrial chemicals
662   Explosives, fuels, related products
663   Beverage technology
664   Food technology
665   Industrial oils, fats, waxes, gases
666   Ceramic and allied technologies
667   Cleaning, color, other technologies
668   Other organic products
669   Metallurgy
670   **Manufactures**
671   Metal manufactures
672   Ferrous metals manufactures
673   Nonferrous metals manufactures
674   Lumber, cork, wood technologies
675   Leather & fur technologies
676   Pulp & paper technology
677   Textiles
678   Elastomers and their products
679   Other products of specific materials
680   **Manufacture for instruments**
681   Precision and other instruments
682   Small forge work
683   Hardware & household appliances
684   Furnishing & home workshops
685   Weather & fur goods
686   Printing and related activities

687 Clothing
688 Other final products and packaging
689
690 **Buildings**
691 Building materials
692 Auxiliary construction practices
693 Construction in specific materials
694 Wood construction carpentry
695 Roofing
696 Utilities
697 Heating, ventilating, air-conditioning
698 Detail finishing
699

THE ARTS

700 The Arts
701 Philosophy & theory
702 Miscellany
703 Dictionaries & encyclopedias
704 Special topics of general applicability
705 Serial publications
706 Organizations & management
707 Study & teaching
708 Galleries, museums, art collections
709 Historical & geographical treatment
710 **Civic & landscape art**
711 Area planning (Civic art)
712 Landscape design
713 Landscape design of trafficways
714 Water features
715 Woody plants
716 Herbaceous plants
717 Structures
718 Landscape design of cemeteries
719 Natural landscapes
720 **Architecture**
721 Architectural construction
722 Ancient & Oriental architecture

723   Medieval architecture
724   Modern architecture
725   Public structures
726   Buildings for religious purposes
727   Buildings for education & research
728   Residential buildings
729   Design & decoration
730   **Plastic Art — Sculpture**
731   Processes & representations
732   Nonliterate, Ancient, Oriental
733   Greek, Etruscan, Roman
734   Medieval sculpture
735   Modern sculpture
736   Carving & carvings
737   Numismatics & sigillography
738   Ceramic arts
739   Art metalwork
740   **Drawing, decorative & minor arts**
741   Drawing and drawings
742   Perspective
743   Drawing & drawings by subject
744
745   Decorative & minor arts
746   Textile arts & handicrafts
747   Interior decoration
748   Glass
749   Furniture & accessories
750   **Painting and paintings**
751   Processes & forms
752   Color
753   Abstractions, symbolism, legend
754   Subjects of everyday life
755   Religion & religious symbolism
756   Historical events
757   Human figures and their parts
758   Other subjects
759   Historical & geographical treatment
760   **Graphic Arts — Prints**

798 Equestrian sports & animal racing
799 Fishing, hunting, shooting

800 LITERATURE (BELLES-LETTERS)

800 **Literature (Belles-letters)**
801 Philosophy & theory
802 Miscellany abut literature
803 Dictionaries & encyclopedias
804
805 Serial publications
806 Organizations
807 Study & teaching
808 Rhetoric & collections
809 History, description, critical appraisal
810 **American Literature in English**
811 Poetry
812 Drama
813 Fiction
814 Essays
815 Speeches
816 Letters
817 Satire & humour
818 Miscellaneous writings
819
820 **English & Anglo-Saxon literatures**
821 English Poetry
822 English Drama
823 English Fiction
824 English Essays
825 English Speeches
826 English Letters
827 English Satire & humour
828 English Miscellaneous writings
829 Anglo-Saxon (Old English)
830 **Literatures of Germanic languages**
831 German Poetry
832 German Drama
833 German Fiction
834 German Essays

835 German Speeches
836 German Letters
837 German Satire & humour
838 German Miscellaneous writings
839 Other Germanic literatures
840 Literatures of Romance languages
841 French Poetry
842 French Drama
843 French Fiction
844 French Essays
845 French Speeches
846 French Letters
847 French Satire & humour
848 French Miscellaneous writings
849 Provençal & Catalan
850 Italian, Romanian, Rhaeto-Romanic
851 Italian Poetry
852 Italian Drama
853 Italian Fiction
854 Italian Essays
855 Italian Speeches
856 Italian Letters
857 Italian Satire & humour
858 Italian Miscellaneous writings
859 Romanian & Rhaeto-Romanic
860 Spanish & Portuguese literatures
861 Spanish Poetry
862 Spanish Drama
863 Spanish Fiction
864 Spanish Essays
865 Spanish Speeches
866 Spanish Letters
867 Spanish Satire & humour
868 Spanish Miscellaneous writings
869 Portuguese
870 Italic literatures — Latin
871 Latin Poetry
872 Latin dramatic poetry & drama

873   Latin epic poetry & fiction
874   Latin lyric poetry
875   Latin speeches
876   Latin Letters
877   Latin Satire & humour
878   Latin Miscellaneous writings
879   Other Italic languages
880   **Hellenic literatures — Greek**
881   Classic Greek poetry
882   Classic Greek drama
883   Classic Greek epic poetry
884   Classic Greek lyric poetry
885   Classic Greek speeches
886   Classic Greek letters
887   Classic Greek satire & humour
888   Miscellaneous writings
889   Modern Greek
890   **Literatures of other languages**
891   East Indo-European & Celtic
892   Afro-Asiatic (Hamito-Semitic)
893   Hamitic & chad literatures
894   Ural-Altaic, Paleosiberian, Dravidian
895   Sino-Tibetan & other Asian
896   African literatures
897   North American native literatures
898   South American native literatures
899   Other literatures

900 GENERAL GEOGRAPHY AND HISTORY AND THEIR AUXILIARIES

900   **General geography & history**
901   Philosophy of general history
902   Miscellany of general history
903   Dictionaries of general history
904   Collected accounts of events
905   Serials on general history
906   Organizations of general history
907   Study & teaching of general history

908
909 General world history
910 **General geography Travel**
911 Historical geography
912 Graphic representations of earth
913 Geography of ancient world
914 Europe
915 Asia
916 Africa
917 North America
918 South America
919 Other areas & worlds
920 **General biography & genealogy**
921
922
923
924
925
926
927
928
929 Genealogy, names, insignia
930 **General history of ancient world**
931 China
932 Egypt
933 Palestine
934 India
935 Mesopotamia & Iranian Plateau
936 Northern & western Europe
937 Italian peninsula & adjacent areas
938 Greece
939 Other parts of ancient world
940 **General history of Europe**
941 British Isles
942 England & Wales
943 Central Europe — Germany
944 France
945 Italy

946 Iberian Peninsula — Spain
947 Eastern Europe — Soviet Union
948 Northern Europe — Scandinavia
949 Other parts of Europe
950 **General history of Asia**
951 China and adjacent areas
952 Japan and adjacent islands
953 Arabian Peninsula and adjacent areas
954 South Asia India
955 Iran (Persia)
956 Middle East (Near East)
957 Siberia (Asiatic Russia)
958 Central Asia
959 Southeast Asia
960 **General history of Africa**
961 North Africa
962 Egypt & Sudan
963 Ethiopia (Abyssinia)
964 Northwest coast & offshore islands
965 Algeria
966 West Africa & offshore islands
967 Central Africa & offshore islands
968 Southern Africa
969 South Indian Ocean islands
970 **South Indian Ocean islands**
971 Canada
972 Middle America — Mexico
973 United States
974 Northeastern United States
975 Southeastern United States
976 South Central United States
977 North Central United States
978 Western United States
979 Great Basin & Pacific Slope
980 **General history of South America**
981 Brazil
982 Argentina
983 Chile

2

Classification

Class + Fication   =   The process of division

=   Divisionisation

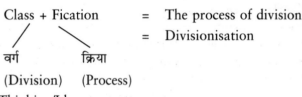

वर्ग   क्रिया

(Division)   (Process)

1. Thinking/Idea

1st Stage — Homogeneous groups (colour, size, length etc.)

2nd Stage — Likeness/unlikeness

Term — Latin "Classic".

First used in Ancient Rome to divide the group of persons.

Two groups: (1) Rich and Poor

(2) Masters and slaves.

This grouping was done on the basis of social structure.

Knower — Knowledge of Entities and concepts.

(The person who   (Specific characteristics of
seeks knowledge)   knowledge)

Knower is man as he has —

  (a) Mind (understanding expression)

  (b) Thinking (perceive the knowledge and apply his mind)

  (c) Extension of thinking (Retrieve the thoughts)

When knower knows something or have knowledge of something, knowledge is established.

Knower — Observes, applies sources and establishes the knowledge.

Knowledge established because:

   (a) Man lives for long period (long life).

   (b) Lives upto three generations of his family (knowledge preserved upto 3 generations).

   (c) Man has ability to reason and analyses — hence, increases the stock of knowledge (extends the knowledge).

Knowers	Things	Concepts
Aristotle	Table	Democracy
Newton————————	Penicillin ———	Relativity
Keats ————————	Stars	——— Love
Gandhi ————————	Books	——— Non-Violence
ǀ	ǀ	ǀ
etc.	etc.	etc.

CLASSIFICATION

Natural   –   According to nature's plan
(Division by nature)   According to nature's order
(Idea Plane)   It is objective classification
                         It is for General purpose

e.g. Earth, sky, stars, animals, man, sea, day, night, plans, fire, instruments, relations.

Artificial   –   According to man
(verbal + Notational)   It is purposeful of individual concerned
                          It is for specific purpose.

e.g. Zeology, Astronomy, Geology, Human society, Oceonology, time, days, months, Botany, Physics, Engg., Customs,

= Every phenomenon, when verbally established and termed in verbal language, becomes a class (subject).

Mill worked out the separate sequence for classification

1. Age and grade of reader (Choice of readers)
2. Book of reference
3. Current books
4. Reserve books
5. Size of documents
6. Physical considerations — Film, cassettes
7. Factual literature (purposeful)
8. Imaginative literature
9. Language
10. Document of temporary significance
11. Rare material (value of document)
12. Form of presentation (Bound periodicals)
13. Date of Printing (Periodicity)
14. Textbooks
15. Document of different sexes
16. Documents of abnormal readers (Blinds).

Specific Subject

It is a piece of knowledge.

Each document is a piece of knowledge.

Each piece of knowledge may be a wider area or minor area within the universe of knowledge.

Categories

1. Simple specific subject (Textbooks : psychology)
2. Compound specific subject (Abnormal psychology)
3. Complex specific subject (Abnormal psychology in relation to social customs).

Basis of Classification

1. To put documents in helpful sequence.
2. To put the documents of small unit of knowledge within the bigger unit of knowledge.
3. To put the coordinate wants of knowledge in an array.

4. To put the subordinate units of knowledge in a chain.

5. To indicate various types of relations between the units of knowledge which is particular traditional basic class.

6. To put various types of relations between more than one basic class.

7. To indicate the relation between special units of knowledge and the common unit found in knowledge.

8. To indicate physical features (vols.).

9. To arrange the documents in a line and in helpful manner.

Ranganathan

Dissection: Divide something in smaller pieces, area etc.

Subdivision by dissection

Example: Universe of Plants

Flowering Plants   Non-flowering plants

(They are in array)

3

Information Generation

Totality of ideas constitutes the universe of subjects. As the universe of ideas develops, the universe of subject also develops and with the development of subject, new subjects are formed.

There are different modes of formation of subjects. Ranganathan postulated four modes in 1950. There are different types of modes for simple, compound and complex subjects.

Simple Subjects

Fission — Means division in smaller pieces. Fission is a process of dividing a Basic subject or fission it or split into sub-divisions of a subject in both the ways. Increasing intention and decreasing extension of subjects in Fission is an internal process. This concept is taken from Atomic Physics in which Nucleus is hit by heavy projection by way of research. It results in very new atoms. Similar process is fission in universe of the subject.

Fission works in three ways:

(a) **Traditional Subjects** — Canonical subject (Basic subjects)

    Example: Mathematics, Physics

                 Mathematics — Algebra

(b) **Fission System** — There are different schools of thought in many subjects which are put under some systems. We call them system fission.

Example: Medical Science
Ayurvedic System
Homeopathy Systems
Allopathy System

(c) **Special Fission** — Every basic subject has some special division having specific characteristics:

Such as – Human being
– Old age
– Childhood
– Adolescence

– Medicine
– Child medicine
– Female medicine
– Tropical medicine.

Types of Fission

There are two types of Fission: 1. Dissection, 2. Denudation.

1. Dissection: Dissection means cutting a universe of entities into parts of coordinate status. Ranganathan has described Dissection in the form of "Array of divisions" of an Isolate or of a Basic class. The classes are remarked equally.

Dissection is the simplest mode of formation of knowledge.

When main class (Basic class) is dissected into several independent classes, it is called Dissection mode.

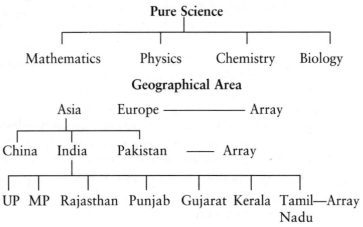

Pure Science

Mathematics   Physics   Chemistry   Biology

Geographical Area

Asia   Europe ——————— Array

China   India   Pakistan ——— Array

UP MP Rajasthan Punjab Gujarat Kerala Tamil—Array
Nadu

2. Denudation: When one and only one division is made by fission mode of formation the basic class and its subdivisions form a chain. It is called Denudation. The extension is decreased and intention is increased.

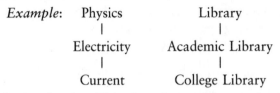

Example: Physics   Library
                 | |
          Electricity   Academic Library
             | |
          Current   College Library

(d) **Lamination:** This gives rise to compound subjects. Under this process, compound subject has layers or lamination over it.

Example:

1. Disease of Lungs = Lungs + Disease (one layer)
2. Treatment of Lungs disease = Lungs + Disease + Treatment. (Two layers)

University Education in India =

Education – Basic Class
University Education =
Education – <u>University</u> (one isolate facet)
Curriculum of University Education =
Education – University – Curriculum
(2 isolate facets)

(e) **Loose Assemblage:** Modern age is an inter-disciplinary research. Two or more subjects or different problems based on different subjects are taken for research, it needs a proper assemblage between the two. It means each subject should have its place but both may produce a thought reflected or effected by both subjects. Subjects may be simple or compound and studies are conducted on their mutual relationship. The relation may be general, bias, comparison, difference and influence. Out of the two subjects one subject may be a tool. Such subject-phase relation resulted to a complex subject.

It is an assemblage of two or more subjects or say basic compound isolate idea.

Example:

> Geo-politics
> Geo-physics
> Socio-psycho study
> Political history
> Philosophy and religion
> Influence of Buddhism over Jainism
> Comparison between Political and Economic geography.
> Astro-Physics (Fusion)
> Astronomy & Physics (Loose Assemblage).

(f) **Distillation**: When main subject is diverse to a compound subject after a process of experience distillation or action-distillation and going with different host basic subject or compound subject, it is called distilled subject. Recent trend in research has resulted in Distillation subjects.

Example:

> Management of College
> Management of Corporates
> Classification of Industries
> Public health programmes of Municipal Corporations.

(g) **Partial Comprehension (Agglomeration)**: It is related to main subject recognized and enumerated in the schedule. This mode is used in some partial context. Usually in context of main class or the subject of filiatory order.

Natural Science — AA-L

It is comprehending more than two main classes in CC, DC.

Humanities — N–S
Social Sciences — T–Z
A is Agglomeration class
It devotes all the sciences.
Pure Science — Maths, Physics, Chemistry etc.
Biological Science — Zoology, Botany, Animal Husbandry, Agriculture etc.

(h) **Cluster:** It is also known as "Subject-Bundle". In this mode a new kind of relation is formed.

Problem — Needs a study of many subjects.
Example: Water problem in Delhi.

It will include the study of:

Various subjects *i.e.*
Geological problem
Pollution problems
Filtering/purifying problem
Supply of water
Demand for water
Water management

Thus, an account of different subjects is brought together out of exigency without any substantial integral account of them. This results in cluster.

4

Forms of Information

1. Main subjects
2. Basic subject
3. Compound subject
4. Complex subject
5. Specific subjects (Isolates)
6. Coordination subjects (array)
7. Subordinate subjects (chain)
8. Subject by system (system)
9. Subject by specials (specials)

RULES OF PRACTICAL CLASSIFICATION

There is a universal explosion of knowledge and libraries are building their collection out of the vast knowledge to feed their readers. The collection has various nature, size, subject and it is to be presented before the readers at one place immediately. Classification is a system which arranges the books in a filiatory sequence. There are several classification systems with their specific character. But every classification scheme deals with the following factors —

1. The title of the book
2. Contents of the book

These two aspects are the basis of classification. The title of book has many characteristics, *i.e.*

1. The words which are relevant
2. The words which are partly related
3. The words which are irrelevant

The points 1 and 2 are considered for the classification purpose. Sometimes the title is neither relevant nor irrelevant, but confusing or not understandable by the classifier.

Example: Study of the man?
             Man?
             Beauty?
             Mind?
             Forwarding a head?
             Reach the sky?

All these titles are not clearly presented by the subject. In such cases the classifier has to consult the thought contents of the book, its content pages, preface, introduction and the reference sources. There are a few documents which are to be consulted in full to decide the subject. There are many chances that the classifier may have to consult the subject experts to reach the subject of the documents.

Classifier is supposed to be a person of vast knowledge, jack of all and a person of academic test so that he may reach to the conclusion to decide the subject.

The second stage is the construction of class number. It is done according to standard schemes of classification, which are internationally known, *e.g.*:

Colon Classification
Dewey Decimal Classification
Universal Decimal Classification
Library of Congress Classification and many others.

BASIC PRINCIPLES

1. The document should be put in the subject which is the need of the reader. In other words the book should have a class number which is the first approach of the reader.

2. The subject should be decided on the basis of the contents:

  (i) Specific subject
  (ii) Nature of the subject
  (iii) Form of the subject

Example: History of Mathematics
          History of Philosophy

In the above two books there are two aspects:

History (of) Mathematics
History (of) Philosophy

Specific Class — Associated subject (form)

Main subject — Mathematics
Form of subject — History

Example: Mathematics + History point of view
          Philosophy + History point of view

3. Subject should be picked up after a serious thought and after going through various characteristics of the relevant discipline. Wrong selection of subject may confuse the reader and make the document, a waste paper item.

4. One book may have more than one subject. The prime and popular should be given the first preference above all other subjects. The subject of the second preference, if warranted, may be added to the prime subject.

5. Sometimes there are two subjects of similar nature. The subject, which is more common and fulfils the nature and objects of a library should be put first.

6. The subject should speak the intention of the author. In other words the angle of the author should be considered.

7. If the classification scheme has not made provision of the specific subject of the document, the near subject number should be given to such books.

8. All the problems experienced in selecting a subject should be recorded for future guidance.

9. The classics, and original books particularly the literary books should be put along with their criticism, terminology, guides, translations, case studies etc.

10. Class number should be constructed on the basis of schedule part and rule part. Index should be consulted only in case of difficulties found in constructing the class number.

HOW TO USE D.D.C.

Headings — Every title represents the subject heading which may be common or specific. We should categorise them as follows:

Large subject

Specific subject

<u>Or</u>   Large subject → Coordinate subject

<u>Or</u>   Specific subject → Associated subject

<u>Or</u>   Specific subject → Parallel subject

<u>Or</u>   Specific subject → Subordinate subject

Example:

[Library] and [Information Science]
[Indian] [Philosophy]
[Spanish] [Language]

Symbols used in D.D.C.

There are a few signs which are used by Dewey Decimal Classification.

1. Square bracket: It is used for two purposes:

(a) Unassigned class number =

There occurs few class numbers which are not assigned.

Example =   006 [Unassigned]
                  008 [Never assigned]

There are empty digits, which may be used, if necessary in revised editions.

So far [Never assigned] class numbers are concerned, they are such which have never been used.

2. [Not to use, class in - - - <.] Such indications are given in Dewey Decimal Classification at many places. They direct not to use, class in - - - means restrictions to use such class number.

Example:

> 747 Interior decoration
> [.09] Historical and geographical treatment
> Do not use, class in 742.2

There is direction (as above) that [.09] is not to be used.

3. **Number discounted**: There are a few places in DDC where directions are given that the said number is restricted for use.

Example:

> 001.6404 Mini computers
> [.64042 – 64044] Analogue and Digital

4. **Optional numbers**: There are a few numbers which are given in square bracket and below it a direction is given "(use of this number is optional, prefer 747.2)".

5. **Asterisk**: There are many places where stars (*) are given with class numbers. It means the directions given in footnotes are to be followed before the direction or digits which are marked* (star).

Example:

> 420–490 specific languages.
> 420* English and Anglo-Saxon language.

---

* Add to base number as instructed under 420-490.

5

Structure of D.D.C.

STRUCTURE: D.C. is a hierarchical system using the Decimal principle for the subdivision of knowledge, as represented in publications; that is, each group in the successive division of knowledge, from the broadest to the most minute, is divided on a base of ten.

The First Division is divided into 10 main classes, 0-9 are used for general works on many subjects from many points of view, such as general newspaper and Encyclopedia and also for certain specialized disciplines that deal with knowledge generally, such as information and communication library science, and journalism.

Main classes 1-9 consist each of a major discipline or group of related disciplines.

10 Main Classes

    0   Generalities
    1   Philosophy and related discipline
    2   Religion
    3   Social Sciences
    4   Languages
    5   Pure Science
    6   Technology (Applied Science)
    7   The Arts
    8   Literature
    9   General geography and history and their auxiliaries

Notation always consists of at least 3 digits, with zero being given its normal arithmetical value where required to fill out a number of 3 digits.

Thus, the full DDC notation for main class, *i.e.* 6 to 600. The notation used to designate the complete span of each main class consists of one hundred. Three digit numbers, *e.g.*, 000-099 for generalities, 300-399 for social science, 600-699 for applied sciences.

MAIN CLASS: Each main class consists of 10 divisions, likewise number 0-9. These division numbers occupy the second position in the notation. Division 0 is needed for general works on the entire main class.

1-9 for such classes of the main class. Thus 6 0 is devoted to general works on the applied sciences,

6 1 is Medical sciences,

6 2 is Engg. and applied operations,

6 3 is Agriculture and related technology.

The full DDC notations for these divisions, each filled out by the addition of a 0, are 600 for General works on main class 6, 610 for Medical Sciences, 620 for Engineering, 630 for Agriculture.

AGAIN each division has a capability of having 10 sections, also numbered 0-9, the section number occupies the third position in the notation. Thus the full span of section numbers for each division listed above is 600 – 609, 610 – 619, 620 – 629, 630 – 639.

In the sections, the 0 in the third position is the number applied to general works on the entire division, and 1-9 are used for sub-classes. Thus —

630 – to Agriculture
631 – to crops and their production
632 – to plant injuries
633 – to killed crops
636 – to animal husbandry

The system permits further subdivision to any degree desired, with a continued decimal notation, which consists of the addition, following any set of three digits as may be required. Thus 636 Animal husbandry is divided into 636.1 Horses and other equines, 636.2 Cattle, 636.3 Sheep, 636.4 Swine, 636.5 Poultry, 636.6 other birds, 636.7 Dogs, 636.8 Cats, 636.9 other warm blooded animals.

636.1 is further divided into 636.11 oriented horses, 636.12 race horse, 636.16 powers, 636.18 other equines such as mules.

> *i.e.*   Main class
> Divisions
> Sections
> Sub-sections lesser degree of specified.

The work 'class' is used to refer to a main class, or a sub-division of any degree, be it 300 or 330, or 338 or 338.47669.

The Concept of Discipline

It is a branch of knowledge of learning. The primary arrangement of DDC is by discipline, by a main and subordinate classes, or:

> Subject,
> Concrete subject,   Not necessarily limited to one
> Abstract concepts,   field of study, are secondary
> Activities or
> Processes.

A subject may appear in any or all of the disciplines.

> Marriage   306   in Sociology
> 155   in Psychology
> 173   in Ethics
> 392   in Custom
> 613   in Hygiene

Hierarchy — The DDC is basically hierarchical in its notation and in its structure.

Notation

1. At each level there is an array of concepts called classes, which are:
   (a) Mutually exclusive.
   (b) Stand in a coordinate relationship to each other.

2. With each new level the specificity of the subject sub-division increases, that is, the classes get progressively more specific, more minute.

3. A given class can be coordinate with one or more other classes of the same level.

<u>Hierarchical Chain – (General to specific)</u>

600	Technology (Applied Sciences)
630	Agriculture & related Technology
636	Animal Husbandry
636.1	Horses
<u>636.12</u>	Race horses

<u>The Digit 0</u> — The digit 0 when not in terminal position distorts the hierarchy but provides a device for extending numbers.

It is generally used to indicate a different basis for division of discipline or subject represented by the digits preceding the 0. In the following sequence 599.01 – .09 are used for general treatment of mammals as a group, whereas 599.1 – .9 are used for works on specific kinds of mammals.

500	Pure Science
590	Zoological Sciences
599	Mammalia
599.01	Physiology of Mammals
599.02	Pathology of Mammals
599.2	Marsupialia
599.8	Primates

Auxiliary tables and Memory aids — Memory aids are mnemonics. The auxiliary tables in this volume form the basis for much of the number building that results to uniform meaning.

6

Use of 'Zero'

1. Common subdivisions are additions to an appropriate simple subject to make it complex.
2. If we have to write number of a class and standard subdivisions, these have to be put in the right order.
3. Standard subdivision, is always a subdivision of other than regular class in schedule.
4. It usually represents an aspect of class number.
5. It can never stand first.
6. It must always come after a class number.

Use of '0'

1. When we add a standard subdivision to a class number that already ends in 0 we must take away the surplus zeros. But one <u>zero</u> must be left to indicate that a common subdivision is being used. Otherwise, resulting number may be confused.

Example: Medical Journal =

$$
\begin{array}{ll}
\text{Medicine} & = \ 610 \\
\text{Journal} & = \ \underline{05} \\
& \ \ \ \ 610.5 \ (\text{Not } 615)
\end{array}
$$

Explanation – 610.05. There is no surplus zero, hence one 0 will be used = 610.5.

2. When DC gives instructions sometimes on the use of standard subdivisions, when a class number ends with 0. Unless there is a contrary instructions there is never any need to use more than a single <u>zero</u> to indicate a standard subdivision,

so that already existing <u>zeros</u> may be deleted until only a single <u>zero</u> remains.

Example: Theory of education —
               Education   370
               Theory & Philosophy   <u>01</u>
                                      370.01

        = 370.1

A history of Technology —
               Technology   = 600
               History   = <u>09</u>
                                     600.09

        = 600.9

3. The whole of the standard subdivision should not be used including the dash —. The dash is to show only that the standard subdivision should be added to a class number from the schedules. Always leave out the dash and add the rest of the standard subdivision as shown in the list.

Example: Case study in Library Ref. Service —

        Library Science   = 020
        Reference Service   = 025.52
        Case Study – 0722

                             = 025.520722

4. We can use standard subdivisions anywhere if DC has no special instructions and they use the single zero shown in the table of standard subdivisions, if DC instructs.

Example: Dictionary of cats —

        Cat – 636.8
        Dictionary = 636.8003

D.C. Page 636:   <u>8003</u> – .<u>8009</u> standard subdivisions
                  Notation from Table 1.

Example:

1. Patents for Library Equipments =   Equipments
                Physical Plants of Library 022.9
                (Equipment)
                Patents – 0272 =   022.90272

2. Theory & Philosophy of Public Administration:
Public Administration = 350
Theory & Philosophy 0001
(In schedule of 351 as per 350.0001
instructions in 350)

Use of more than two zero 1001-009 in Standard Subdivisions

1. If at any given number there are subdivisions having a notation beginning with zero '0', use 001-009 for standard subdivisions.

2. If notations beginning with zero '0' and 00 both have special purposes, use 0001-0009 for standard subdivisions.

Example: 3 3 0 — One zero

Use 330.001
335.001 →35–009

Every standard subdivision begins with a zero. But when adding the standard subdivision to a class number you have to see —

1. Whether the class number is free to take the standard subdivision with one zero.

2. In certain cases already a number would have been enumerated with one zero standing for some other concepts.

Example: 027.01 would mean used libraries.

It would not mean 'Philosophy and theory' as 01 here is not the standard subdivision number. It is used for Geographical treatment. And if we want to represent philosophy and theory of general libraries, then your number will be 027.001. Note the two zero '00' in this class number.

7

Table – 1
Standard Subdivisions

Subject is a basis of classification, but its presentation is important so as to help the reader to trace the books. Books are published in different forms and angles. Some books are based on scientific principles but a few are just put or grown as a general subject. There are many angles of a subject —

1. Historical point of view
2. Psychological point of view
3. Scientific point of view
4. Information point of view
   etc. etc.

Books have many forms —

1. Macro-thought — Books or books like
2. Micro-thoughts — Periodicals and periodical likes

Standard subdivisions are applied to all subjects. They are common to all.

Example: Dictionary
                   Encyclopedia
                   Periodicals
                   Bibliographies
                   Essays etc.

The schedule of such standard subdivisions are given in Volume 1 of DDC. The nomenclature of common isolates have been changed from time to time in different editions of DDC.

Important Standard Subdivisions

–01 Philosophy and theory

–02 Miscellany

–03 Dictionary, encyclopedias, concordance

–04 Special topics of general applicability

–05 Serial publications

–06 Organization and Management

–07 Study and teaching

–08 History and description of the subject among groups of persons

–09 Historical and Geographical treatment.

Standard subdivisions has no separate existence. Their value and importance is identified when they are used or attached to any subject. They sharpen the subject and extend it to more specific character. Every standard subdivision is represented with — as to show the gap of the class number to be filled up before the standard subdivision.

Example:

1. – 01 Philosophy and Theory

    ↓

    This gap is to be filled up by a subject number.

2. Theory of Banking:

$$\underset{\text{Economics} \qquad \text{Philosophy and theory}}{3\,3\,2\,.\,0\,1}$$

Every standard subdivision starts with zero '0'.

1. Other form of subject

Categories:

(a) Synopsis

(b) Outlines

(c) Serial publications

(d) Collection of letters/essays

(e) Schedule or table

(f) Pictures / photographs

All these types of subdivisions are included in Table 1.

2. Inner form of subject

There are many subjects which have similar entities, *e.g.*:

(a) Principles

(b) Techniques

(c) History

(d) Study and teaching

All these subdivisions are included in Table 1.

3. Subdivisions other than outer forms and inner forms

There are a few standard subdivisions which represent the activities and techniques of a subject and also work as indicators or guides or directions in which digits are added.

Example:

Textbooks [of] Chemistry for nurses

Mathematics for engineers

= –024 works for specific types of users.

The users are added from Table 7.

Nature of Standard Subdivisions

1. Standard subdivisions are added to the end of the class number of the document in question. Standard subdivisions are not unnecessarily invited to add with specific class.

Example:

Encyclopedia of Islam: 297 + 03 = 297.03

History of Ahmadia Movement: 297.86 + 09 = 297.8609

2. Subjects whose specific class number does not exist in schedule should not be expanded by adding a standard sub-division. In other words, if a specific class number of a subject is not available in the schedule, such subject should not be expanded by adding subdivisions.

Examples:

Standards for goat milk

Milk production   –   637.1

3. There is no specific subject 'standard' in the schedules.

All other milks are   –   637.17

— Hence, the final number will be 637.17, Not 637.170218

This will be done because —

(a) Further expansion is not needed if the near number is available and actual number is not available in the schedule.

(b) Unnecessary adding of subdivision may confuse the reader and mislead his thinking.

4. It is rare occasion when two standard subdivisions are appended to the number of the subject. If number demands two standard subdivisions, only one is to be applied, the other ignored.

5. The classification must always bear in mind that the focus of a work is more important than the instructions from the classification.

6. If we examine the preferential order for table 1 and focus is not obvious, it becomes obvious that —

(a) The general special concepts are followed by view point and

(b) then by the physical form.

(c) Internal forms are to be preferred over external forms and genuine subdivision of the topic (04) preferred overall.

Example:

Encyclopedia of organization that deal with applied psychology

– Encyclopedia and organization concepts are presented by standard subdivision 03 and 0601–0609

– Only one may be added

– Preferable table or is to be given preference over 03

– Therefore current number is 158.06, Not 153.03

Directory of library schools in India

         020.71154, NOT 020.2554

Use of more than two zeros in standard subdivisions

1. If at any given number there are subdivisions having a notation beginning with zero "0", use 001–009 for standard subdivisions.

2. If notations begin with zero '0' and '00' both have special purposes:

Use 0001–0009 for standard subdivisions.

The classes enumerated in the schedule can be divided into two categories from the point of view of the use of standard subdivisions:

1. Classes under which instruction for use of standard subdivision is provided.

2. Classes where no instruction is provided.

With instruction: .001–.008 Notation from Table 1.

Example:

Philosophy of library relations = 021.001

Without instructions:

Example: Philosophy of library evaluation – 021.01

Philosophy of library classification–025.42 + 01

= 025.4201

Use of '0' of standard subdivision

1. The number of standard subdivision starts with '0' for —

(i) Physical

(ii) View-point

2. When the number already ends with '0'.

3. Unless there are instructions, there is no need to use more than a single '0' to indicate standard subdivision, and that already existed '0' (zero) may be deleted until only a single zero remains.

Example:

The philosophy of education

Philosophy	=	01
Education	=	370

370.1 NOT 370.01

The history of Technology :

Technology	=	6<u>00</u>
History	=	<u>09</u>
		600.9 NOT 600.09

Essays on Architecture:

Architecture	=	720
Essays	=	<u>08</u>
		720.8 NOT 720.08

4. Standard subdivision may be added to any class number in a division or section, that is end with two or one '0'.

Example

Encyclopedia of Science

Science	=	5<u>00</u>
Encyclopedia	=	<u>03</u>
		503

Journal of Philosophy:

$$1\underline{00} + 05 = 105$$

(In case of 3 zeros, fill the gap and put '.' After 3 digits.)

Philosophy of Maths = $51\underline{0} + 01 = 510.1$

5. When the normal standard subdivision position has been occupied by a subject division —

Example:

Dictionary of Social Science:

Social Sciences	=	3<u>00</u>
Dictionary	=	<u>03</u>
		300.3

Other Examples:

Journal of Fluid Mechanic = 532.05 NOT 532.005
Journal of Dynamics 532.0505 NOT 532.05005
Research in statistics 530.02072 NOT 532.020072
Lib. & Inf. Science profession 020.23
Indian History through pictures 954.00222
Indian Library Association 020.62254
University imparting library
Science education in Maharashtra State 020.71154792

Collected biography for librarians 020.922
Child psychology for parents 155.40240431
Math. Statistics for librarians 5195024092

6. One standard subdivision should not be added to another standard subdivision.

Example: Patents for scale models of library equipments

Library equipment	022.9
Patents	0272
Scale model	0228

= 022.9 + 0272 = 022.90272

NOT 022.902280272

7. If there is already readymade number mentioned in the schedule, <u>Do not</u> construct a number for the same subject by using the standard subdivision.

Example: Dictionary of Bible = 220
(Do not use Standard subdivision for Dictionary)
    NOT = 220.03
Agriculture tool Machinery   631.3
                <u>NOT</u>   631.028

8. Under certain classes in schedule, the standard subdivisions are expanded and these are known as extended standard subdivisions. These <u>extended</u> subdivisions are to be used only for the class.

Example:

<u>Table 1</u> = <u>Student, learners, apprentices</u>   073

If applied to 610 its meaning is expended to meaning "Study teaching nursing", related technology.

=   610.73 (61<u>0</u> + 073 = 610.73)

<u>Table 1</u> = Freedom, dignity and value of labour 013
        Labour economics   331
        Dignity of labour   331.013

9. Every standard subdivision begins with zero. When adding the standard subdivision to a class number, it is to be seen:

(a) Whether class number is free to take the standard subdivision with one '0'.

(b) In certain cases, a number is already enumerated with one '0' standing for other concept.

Example:

1. World libraries   027.01

(Here '01' does not represent standard subdivision)

Here it is not used as standard subdivision.

It is for Geographical treatment.

But if added standard subdivision:

01–Philosophy and theory. The Number will be 027.001

2. Theory and philosophy of public administration

350 + 0001 = 350.0001

3. Journal of the Central Government

351 + 0005 = 351.0005

10. If the ultimate class number, to which standard subdivision is to be added, is a <u>main class ending with two zeros '00'</u> or a <u>division ending with one zero '0'</u>. Then —

(a) Delete two zeros in the first case.

(b) Delete one zero in the second case.

e.g. Encyclopedia of literature

8 + 03 = 803

(Two zeros from 8<u>00</u> are deleted)

Journal of Economics

33<u>0</u> + 05 = 330.5

(One zero from 33<u>0</u> is deleted)

11. There are certain subjects —

(a) Which have no specific class number

(b) These are usually classified under broad subjects.

<u>Such subjects</u> should not be expended by standard subdivisions.

e.g. = Govt. Milk has no specific class number.

Hence, it has to be classified under 537.17.

In Standards of Goat milk, standard subdivision will be added and the number of the main subject 537.17 stands.

Examples:

1. Theory of Dewey Decimal Classification
   025.431 + 01 = 025.43101

2. Scientific principles of UDC
   025.432 + 015 = 025.432015

Rule .015. Add to the base number, the number following in 510–590

Mathematical principles – 0151

Example: Mathematical principles of library classification
025.42 + 015 + 1 (following 5 from 510)
= 025.420151

Index to Library Classification
= 025.42 + 16 = 025.42016

Examples:

1. Apparatus and equipment for description cataloguing
   025.32028

2. Library and Information Science Profession   020.23

3. Acronyms in Library and Information Science   020.148

4. Indian history through pictures   954.00222

5. History of Mughal India through pictures 954.0250222

6. Indian Library Association   020.62254

7. Research in Library Classification in
   Canada   025.42072071

8. Collected biography for librarians   020.922

9. History of Philosophy in India   109.54
   (Not Indian Philosophy)

10. Child Psychology for parents   155.40240431

11. Outlines of Colon Classification   025.4350202

12. Standards for library buildings   022.30218

13. Plans and diagrams of lib. building   022.30223

14. Library Science as a hobby   020.23
                                                   (020.023)

15. Statistics for librarians
$$519.5 + 02 + 092 = 029.5024092$$

16. Testing of library equipments
$$0229 + 0287 = 022.90287$$

17. Dictionaries of Library and Information Science
$$02 + 03 = 020.3$$

18. Journal of Library Science $\quad 02 + 060 + 54 = 020.6054$

19. Reference service among doctors
$$025.52 + 088 + 61 = 025.5208861$$

20. Reading interests of Indians
$$028.55 + 089 = 91411 = 028.5508991411$$

21. Theory and philosophy of library relations
$$021 + 001 = 021.001$$

12. In subject Library and Information Science, instructions are given to add numbers with two or three zeros under the following class numbers:

```
022.3301 – 3305
025.001 – 009
025.460001 – 460009
026.0001 – .0009
027.001 – .008
```

Examples:

1. Encyclopedia of public finance $336 + 003 = 336.003$

2. Study and teaching of Pediatrics
   $618.92 + 0007 = 618.920007$

3. Directory of Public finance of Ohio
   $356 + 025771 = 336.25771$

4. Cardiology journal
   $616.12 + 005 = 616.120005$

5. Foreign trade of India since 1947
   382.0954009044

6. Foreign trade between India and Australia
   382.0954094

09 HISTORY AND GEOGRAPHIC DIVISION

Add — 09 to the class number without any alteration which gives you a number with two zeros '00'.

1. The Geographical subdivision is important enough to have several places allotted to it and these places end in the digits used already of the beginning of the area notation.

2. Then there is no need to use the same digit twice, or to continue to use the 9 that is often characteristic of Geographical subdivision in D.C.

3. 4–9 are area notations for various countries.

4. If we add 42 for GREAT BRITAIN, there is no need to repeat the 4 already in the class number, so the correct number is 289.342.

8

Table – 2: Area

The most notable memory aid is area arrangement. In nearly all area developments, the digit 44 stands for France, 45 for Italy, 52 for Japan, 73 for U.S.A.

In each case with a decimal point following the third digit.

"Area" specifies area number.

1. Area notations are never used alone,

2. But may he used as required (even directly) when so noted or through the interposition of 'Standard subdivisions' notations 09 from table 1, with any number from the schedule.

e.g.   Wages   = 331.29

Wages in Japan   = (–52 in this table)

                               = 331.2952

Rail road transportation in Brazil = 385.0981

Transportation – 385

Brazil (–81)

(p. 384 - 385.09 Historical & Geog. Treatment)

When adding to a number from the schedules, always insert a decimal point between the third and fourth digits of the complete number.

Area Summary

  –1 Area, region, places in general

  –2 Persons regardless of area, region, place

  –3 The Ancient World

  –4 Europe, Western Europe

–5 Asia Orient for East

–6 Africa

–7 North America

–8 South America

–9 Other parts of world and extra-terrestrial worlds Pacific ocean Islands (Oceania).

–1 **Areas, regions, place in general**

    (a) Not limited by continent, country, locality. If desired, add to each number as follows:

    (b) 03–09 treatment by continent, country, locality.

    (c) Add 0 to base number and then add "Areas" notation 3–9 from this table.

1. **Torrid Zone of Asia**

Torrid zone	=	13
Connect by	=	0
(Add from –3 to –9 from table 2)		
Asia	≡	<u>5</u>
		1305

2. **Rivers of England**

Rivers	=	1693
Connect by	=	0
England	=	42

3. **Italian speaking region of Switzerland**

Region	=	175
Italian	=	51
Connect	=	0
Switzerland	=	<u>494</u>
		175510494

4. **Cities of ancient Greece – 1732038**

Cities	=	1732
Connect	=	0
Ancient Greece	=	38

Example = Torrid Zone of Area   – 13<u>05</u>,
           River of England   – 1693042,
           Italian-Speaking regions
               of Switzerland   – 175510494
           Cities of ancient Greece – 1732038

(An alternative treatment is shown under 3–9)

= Torrid Zone   – 13 (Area Notation)
  Base Number   – 0 = 130
  Asia   – 5 = 1305

Air and water of Asia = <u>16</u> <u>0</u> <u>5</u>   (Base No. / Asia)

Vegetation forest of Japan = 1 5 2 0 <u>5</u> 2
Rivers of England – 1693<u>0</u>42
Cities of Ancient Greece – 1732<u>03</u>8

Unless instructions are given, class complexity defines areas with aspects in two or more subdivisions of this area table in the number coming last in the states.

e.g. Forested plateaus in Northern Temperate Zone — 152

(Not – 123 or – 143)

Number 1 and its subdivisions stand for various zones, like Temperate Zones, Frigid Zones etc.

Land and Land formation – Island, Mountains
Regions by Vegetation   – Forests, Grasslands.
Air and Water Formation – Atmospheres, Oceans, Seas.
Socio-Economic regions   – Western Block, Communistic Block

Non-Aligned Countries
Eco-Backward Area
Aryan Countries
Slavic Countries
English Speaking Countries

It is very odd number in the table covering persons, regardless of area, region and place.

When there are instructions to add "Areas" notation 1–9 directly from table 2 instead of adding "Standard Subdivisions" notation 091-099 from Table 1, classify here description and critical appraisal of work, biography, autobiography, diaries, renaissance — 372.92 Elementary Educators.

Example

1. Social Science in Bible
   Bible = 220.8 = Add 001-999 to base number
   Social Science = 3<u>00</u> = 220.83

2. Sciences in Bible = 220.85

3. Marketing of = 658.809 (Marketing of specific kinds
   transformers   of goods and services)
         – (Add 001–999 to base number 658.809)

   Transformers = 621.314
   Class Number = 658.809621.314

4. Classification of Social Sciences
   Classification = 025.46
         = Add 001–999 to base number 025.46
   Social Sciences + 3<u>00</u> = 025.463

Add subdivisions of one main class

Sometimes classifier uses subdivisions of one main class only, under which 'Add' instructions are provided.

Steps

1. Write the base number of the specific subject under which the instructions are given.

2. Verify the main class number whose subdivisions are to be used as per instructions.

3. Write down the class number of the subdivision which is needed from the given main class.

4. Omit or keep in square brackets the class number indicating the main class.

5. Add the remaining number to the base number.

Example:

1. Cooperative milk production
   Cooperative   – 334.68
   334.682 – 689 – Extractive, manufacturing,
   construction.
   (Add to base number 334.68 the numbers following 6
   in 620–690).
   Milk Production – 637.1 = 334.68371

   (Add number following 6 = 6   <u>37.1</u>
                                   ×

2. Unemployment in chemical and allied industries
   Unemployment – 331.137
   Unemployment in specific industries
             331.13781 – 331.13789
   331.13782 – .13789 Extractive, manufacturing,
   construction industries.
   (Add to base number 331.1378 the numbers following
   6 in 620–690).
   Chemical and related technologies = 660
             = 331.13786

Add subdivisions of specific division of Main Class

1. Use the subdivisions of such main division of the given main class which is provided in the instructions. Main class is generally divided in a main division and each of these divisions are further subdivided generally in 9 subdivisions.

Similarly Add Device permits use of the subdivisions of one specific subdivisions of the main division.

Example:

1. Prices of nut fruits – 338.1345
   Prices of specific products 338.13–.138
   (Add to base number 338.13 the numbers following
   63 in <u>633</u>–6<u>38</u>.
   Nut fruits   – <u>63</u>4.5
   338.13<u>45</u>

2. Diseases of respiratory system in old age
   Geriatrics   – 618.97
   Specific disease – .976–.978
   [Add to base number 618.97 the numbers following 61 in 616–618]
   Diseases of respiratory system – 616.2
   Base No. 618.97 – Add numbers following 616.2
   = 618.9762

3. Rites and ceremonies in Jain religion
   Jainism   –   294.4
   General principles   –   294.41 – .48
   [Add to base number 294.4 the numbers following 291 in 291.1 – 291.87]
   Rites and ceremonies   –   291.38
   Base number 294.4   Add number following 291
                                    [291.38]
   = 294.438

4. Library science students organization
   Higher education   –   378
   Physical plant, health and safety, the student 378.196–198
   Add to base No. 378.19 the numbers following 371 in 371.6 – 371.8
   Student organization in specific field = 371.84
   [Add 001–999 to base number 371.84
   020 Library and Information Science
   378.19 [371.84 + 020 = 378.1984020

Add device of some more digits

4 digits

Add numbers following 291.4 in 291.41 – 291.44
                       633.1 in 633.11 – 6333.18

Example:

1. Attitude of Buddhism towards crime —
   Buddhism   294.3
   Relationship and attitude –   294.33
   [Add to base number 294.33 the numbers following 291.1 in 291.13 – 291.17]

Crime   –   291.17833
= 294.33 + [291.1]7833 = 294.337833

2. A study of barley and its products:
641.33 + [333.1]6 = 641.336

5 digits

1. River transportation of passengers
River transportation   386.3
Activities and services   386.35
Transportation of passengers   386.242
(Add numbers following 386.24)
= 386.35 + [386.24]2 = 386.352

2. Urban traffic control and other highway services
Local transportation   388.4
Traffic flow and maintenance   388.4131
(Add base number 388.312–388.314 the numbers
following 388.31 in 388.312–388.314)
Traffic control and other highway services 388.312
388.4131 + [388.31] 2 = 388.41312

6 digits

1. Facilities in commercial aircrafts
Air transportation   387.7
Facilities   387.73
Aircrafts   387.732–.733
(Add those numbers 387.73 the numbers following
629.133 in 629.1332–629.1333)
Airplanes   629.13334
Commercial   629.133340423
= 387.73 + [629.133]340423 = 387.73340423

2. Attitude of Hinduism towards cruelty to animals
Hinduism   294.5
Relationship, doctrine, public works – 294.51–53
(Add to base number 294.5 the numbers following
291 in 291.1–291.3)
Relationships and attitude of religions – 291.1
Crime   291.17833
(Add to base number 291.17833 the numbers following
364 in 364.1 – 364.8)

Cruelty to animals   364.187
Base No. 294.5 + [291].17833 + [364]187 =
294.517833187

Add numbers from table

1. Add device is used to add notations from the table given in Vol. 1 to subdivide a class No.

2. Specific table is also mentioned after the term 'Add' *e.g.* Add 'Areas' notations or Add 'languages' notations or Add 'persons' notations etc.

Examples:

1. Libraries in India

   General libraries   027
   (Add 'Area' notation 1–9 from table 2 to base number 027.0)
   India   –54
   = 027.0 + 54   = 027.054

2. Bengali language collections

   General Collection   080 (Generalia)
   In other languages   089
   (Add 'Languages' notation 2–9 from table 6 to base number 089)
   Bengali – 9144 (Table 6)
   = 089 + 9144   = 089.9144

3. Science journalism – 070.449 + 500
                      = 070.4495

4. Salaries for Engineers 331.281 + 620 = 351.28162

5. Job opportunities in librarianship
   331.1241 + 020 = 331.124102

6. Curriculum in Engg. 375 + 620 = 375.62

7. Agricultural labour 331.38 + 630 = 331.3863

8. Buddhist Philosophy
   181.0 + 43 (from 2943) = 181.043

Examples:

1. Soil preparation for rice
   633.18 + 1 (from 63151) = 633.181
2. Paddy seeds
   633.18 + 21 (from 631.53) = 633.1821
3. Soil preparation of wheat – 633.11 + 1 = 633.111
4. Fungus diseases of paddy plants
   633.18 + 9 + 4 = 633.1894
5. Anatomy Gastropoda –   594.3044
   Genetics of Gastropoda–   594.30415
6. Pathology of Reptilia   –   597.0042
7. Anatomy of invertebrates –   592.04 (from 591.4)
8. President of Pakistan   –
   354.5491 + 0 + 4 = 354.5404
9. Powers of US President
   353.03 + 22 (from 351.00322) = 353.0322
10. Prevention of Tuberculosis
    616.995 + 05 = 616.99505

Area notation is a Geographical division in D.D.C. It is in 373 pages. It is limited to the use of Indo-Arabic numerals from 1–9. Hence 9 has been allotted to Area division.

Under Area Division – 1 is allotted to General Area:

1 – General Area – Area, regions, places in general.

   11 Frigid Zones
   12 Temperate Zone (Middle Latitude Zones)
   13 Torrid Zone (Tropics)
   14 Land and Landforms
   15 Regions by type of vegetation
   16 Air and Water
   17 Socio-Economic regions
   18 Other kinds of terrestrial regions
   19 Spaces

2 – Persons regardless of area, region, place.

For these persons do not use standard subdivisions from table 1.

Classify here description and critical appraisal works, biography, autobiography, diaries, correspondence of persons associated with the subject —

Example: Elementary educators

> 372 – Elementary education
> 92 – Persons of education field

– 22 Collected

– 24 Individual

– 26 Case histories

Alternative number – [Class in area]

Arizona under Mexican Sovereignty

791 – Arizona

– 3 Ancient world

Classify here specific part of ancient world [not provided for here in – 4–9].

(For Modern world class in 4–9)

– 4–9 **The modern world: Extra-terrestrial World**

Class comprehension work on specific physiographic regions or features extending over more than one country, state, country or other units and identified by * with the unit where noted in the table.

Example:

(1) Lake Huron – 744

(2) Libraries in Kashmir – 027.5466

> 027 – Libraries
> .01.09 Geographical treatment
> [Add area notation 1–9 from table 2 to base no. 027.0]
> 54913 – Kashmir
> = 027.054913

(3) Public libraries in Karnataka

027.4 Public libraries

(Add Area notation 3–9 from table 2 to base number 027.4)

    5487   Karnataka

=   027.45487

(4) Elementary schools in Pakistan

    372.00   Elementary Schools

    372.95491   Geographical treatment

(5) Higher education in Andhra Pradesh

    378   Higher education

    378.<u>5484</u>   Andhra Pradesh

(6) Birds in Bhutan – 598.295498

(7) Adult Education in Denmark – 374.9489

(8) Foreign Policy of Ireland – 327.415

(9) Social Laws of New Zealand – 344.31

(10) College Libraries in Spain – 027.746

(11) Algerian Churches in Hungary – 203.439

(12) Hunting in Ancient India – 744.2934

College Libraries in Spain – 027.746

There are three types of directions

1. If we classify a subject under a class number, in some subject there are directions at the end of that class number under .09 *e.g.* 382.09, 331.09.

Example:

   (a) International Commerce – 382   = 382.09

   (b) Labour economics (Industrial relations) 331.54 = 331.0954.

2. If we classify a subject under a class number, there are directions in that subject for Geographical treatment in the end .3–.9 <u>or</u> .4–.9 *e.g.* 378.4–.9, 327.3–.9, 344.3–.9, 346.3–.9.

Example:
- (a) Higher education in India — 378.54
- (b) International relations in India — 327.54
- (c) Social law in India — 344.54
- (d) Private law in India — 346.54

3. There are some subjects in schedule in which 9 is given as the last digit of the subject *e.g.* 361, 362, 363, 364, 365, 366, 367, 368. There are directions under 9 for geographical division.

> *e.g.* 361.9   Historical and Geographical treatment
> 361.91–.99 Geographical treatment
> Add Area notation 1–9 from table 2 to base number 361.9.

Example:
361	Social problems and social welfare
361.9	Historical and geographical treatment
362	Social welfare problems and services
362.9	Historical and Geographical treatment
374	Adult education
374.9	Historical and geographical treatment

There are two types of directions:
- (i) 369
- (ii) 361.9 Historical & Geog. treatment
.91–.99 Geographical treatment.

4. There are a few subjects in which subject numbers are extended upto 9 but there are no directions. The Geographical notation may be added by .09.

> *e.g.* 589.9   Schizomyctes
> 589.9 <u>09</u>   Geographical treatment.

Exception

(A) There are a few exceptions where Geographical division is used by other methods.

> *e.g.* 398.2   Folk literature
> 398.23   Tales and core of places and times
> <u>398.232</u> Real places
> (Add Area notation 1–9 from table 2 to base number 398.232).

Examples:

    (a) Folk-tales of Kashmir – 398.232546

    (b) Administration of local Govt. in Rajasthan – 352.0544

    (c) Industrial research in U.K. – 607.242

(B) Some main subjects class numbers are constructed after subdiving the notations of Modern World in Table 2 of Geographical subdivision.

Main class 910 General geography has a base number 92 which has direction to divide as 4–9 for modern world.

Examples:

910 General Geography Travel	Table 2
914 Geography of and travel in Europe	– 4 Europe
915 Geography of and travel in Asia	– 5 Asia
916 Geography of and travel in Africa	– 6 Africa
917 Geography of and travel in N. America	– 7 N. America
918 Geography of and travel in S. America	– 8 S. America
919 Geography of and travel in other parts	– 9 other parts of the world & extra-terrestrial worlds of the world and extra-terrestrial world.

In such circumstance, if Geography of any country is needed, then the direction for Geographical subdivision should be traced under the continent of such country.

    e.g. Geography of Canada   917.1

[Canada is in North America. Base number of geography is 91. As such the notation of North America is taken from table 2 and thus the number is = 91 – General Geography
                            7 – North America
                        71 – Canada = 917.1]

    Christian Church in China 275.1

    Geography subdivision:

1. Area, regions, places in general

e.g. Physical geography of torrid zone 910.0213

1 is not limited by continent, country, locality.

If desired, add to each number as follows:

03–09 Treatment by continent, country, locality

<u>Add</u> 0 to base number and then add "Area notation 3–9" from this table.

e.g. (a) Torrid zone of Asia   – 1305

   13 Torrid Zone

   0 to be added to base number 13

   5 Asia

   (b) Rivers of England 1693 + 0 + 42 = 1693042

   (c) Italian speaking reasons of Switzerland
   = 1755 + 0 + 494 = 175510494

   (d) Cities of ancient Greece = 1732 + 0 + 38 + 1732038

[There are <u>alternative numbers</u> as shown under – 3–9]

Examples:

   (a) Birds of desert Asia – 598.29 + –154 = 598.29154

   (b) Economic assistance by communist countries
   = 338.911717 = 338.91 + –1717 = 338.911717

   (c) International trade of western block = 382.091713
   = 382.09 + –1713 = 382.091713

If no directions in any manner

If there are no instructions to add area notation for a subject, we can add area notation through standard sub-division – <u>09</u>.

Game of 9

9 in schedule as subject:

351.9	Malfunctioning of governments
368.9	Insurance of specific continents
398.9	Proverbs
554.9	Other economic materials
574.9	Geographical treatment of organism
575.9	Origin and evaluation of sexes

612.9	Regional physiology		
333.9	Other natural resources		
232.9	Family and life of Jesus		
371.9	Special education		
526.9	Surveying		
539.9	Tables, review and exercise		
613.9	Family placing and sex hygiene		
069.9	Museum devoted to specific discipline		
149.9	Other systems of doctrines		
340.9	Conflict of law		

.901–905	Historical periods	330.901–905	Eco. Situation__ period
.91–.99	Geographical treatment	330.91–99	Economic Geography
.09	Historical and Geog. treatment	321.09	Change of form of state
		343.09	Country of public utility
.3–.9	327.3–.9	Foreign policies of and foreign evaluations between specific nations	
	337.3–.9	Foreign Eco. policy and relation of specific jurisdiction and groups of jurisdiction	
	343.3–.9	Specific jurisdiction and areas.	

Specific subdivisions

324.24–.29   Treatment by specific continent, country localities in modern world

328.4–.9   Legislative branch of specific jurisdiction by modern world

546   Inorganic Chemistry

09 in specific subdivisions

328.4–.909   History of Legislative branch of specific jurisdiction

092   Biography.

Area notation through standard subdivision

= 09

If there is no instruction to add area notation for a subject, we can add area notation through standard subdivision 09.

There are directions under 09, to add the number of the area. Thus, the further number may be taken from further geographical subdivision.

Therefore, Geographical subdivision –1 Area region, place in general is taken with 09, *i.e.* 091.

Similarly – 3 Ancient world in – 3–9.

– 4 Modern world in – 4–9.

–093–099 Treatment by specific continents, countries, localities, extra-terrestrial worlds.

– History and description by place, by specific instance of the subject.

Add area notation 3–9 from table 2 to base number –09.

e.g. Subjects in U.S.   – 0973

Subjects in Brazil   – 0981

Subjects in India   – 0954

1. **Class persons** associated with the subjects regardless of area, region, place in – 092.

2. **Treatment of area,** regions, place not limited by continent, country, locality in – 091.

3. **History and description** of the subject among group of specific kinds of persons in – 88.

4. **Among specific racial, ethnic** national group non-document in their continent, countries, localities in – 089.

Examples:

1. Library science in United States   020.973

.020   Library Science
.973   United States

2. Palmistry in Ancient Egypt   131.60932

133.6   Palmistry
–32   Egypt
09   Standard subdivision

= 133.60932

3. Naval forces in Yugoslavia   359.009497

359   Naval forces

(Use 359.001 – 359.009)

09 Standard subdivision
–497 Yugoslavia
= 358.009497

4. Disease of infants in Europe   618.9200094
618.92   Pediatrics
(618.920001 – 618.920009 for standard subdivision)
– 4 Europe
= 618.92 + – 0009 + – 4 = 618.9200094

5. Specific libraries of Romania   026.0009498
026   Libraries devoted to various specific disciplines and subject
(Use 026.0001 – 026.0009 for standard subdivision)
= 026 + 0009 + – 498 = 026.0009498

Other examples:

1. Adult education in rural areas of Kerala
374.9 + 1734 + 0 + 5483 = 374.9173405483

2. Democracy in India and Pakistan
321.80954 or 321.8095491

3. Foreign policy of India towards Iran
327 + 54 + 0 + 55 = 327.54055

4. Immigration from India to Nepal
325.2 + 54 + 09 + 5496 = 325.254095496

5. Trade agreement between India and Bhutan
382.9   –   Trade agreement
54   –   India
0   –   Add notation
5498   –   Bhutan
= 382.95405498

6. History of Central Asia – 958

7. General statistics for Dacca – 315.4922

8. Indian Architecture – 722.44

9. Journalism in Canada – 071.1

10. Political conditions in China in 13th Century

320.9   – Political conditions
51   – China
0   – Add notation
22   – 13th century = 09<u>022</u> 13th century
= 320.951022

11. Indian Income Tax Law = 343 + 54 + 052
12. Prime Minister of China 354 + 51 + 0313
13. Hinduism in <u>Bengali</u> area – 294.509 + 174 + <u>9144</u>
    (Table 6)
14. Book publishing in Spanish speaking countries
          070.509 + 175 + 61 (Table 6)
          = <u>070</u> . <u>509</u> <u>175</u> <u>61</u>

       Journalism   Historical &   Region where specific
                    Geo.   language predominates
                    treatment

Spanish

15. Library relationship in South India – 021.039548
    021   Library relationship
    021.009   Historical and Geographical treatment
    –548   South India
    = 021.009548
16. Library cooperation in Rajasthan = 021.6409545
    021.64   Library cooperation
    (There is no direction for Geographical subdivision)
    Hence it will add <u>09</u> with base number
    – 544 Rajasthan
    021.64.09544
17. Human diseases in West Bengal = 6160095414
    Human   = 600
    Diseases   = 616
                   009 Historical & Geog. treatment

West Bengal   = 5414
               = 616.0095414

18. Tuberculosis disease in Iraq = 616.995009567
616.996   Tuberculosis
(Notation may be added as 616. –616.9 – other
disease)
666.995   Tuberculosis
009   Historical & Geographical treatment
– 567   Iraq
= 666.995.009567

19. Agricultural sociology of underdeveloped countries
= 307.72091724
307.72   Rural Economics
(Direction — Divide Agricultural Sociology in the
same numbers)
–1724   Underdeveloped countries
09 is used as no direction of Geographical treatment
= 307.72091724.

Relation between two countries

There are provision of numbers for relationship between
the two countries. Two countries are added by 0 or 09.

But if there are no directions of relation between two
countries, then two countries should not be taken together.

Preference to which country first?

1. The country in which the book is given more importance.

2. If the book is given importance in both the countries
equally, the country which comes first in the schedule should
be given first.

3. If desired, local place may be given first place, even if it
is later in the schedule.

Example:

1. Foreign relations between India and Japan
= 327.54052
327 – International relations
(.3–.9 foreign policies of and foreign relations between
specific nations from Geographical schedule)

```
54      –  India
0       –  relation symbol
52      –  Japan
=  327.54052
```

2. Foreign trade between Great Britain and United States

```
382.0942073
382 – International Commerce
```

(.09 Historical & Geographical treatment)
```
382.09
```
(1–9 is taken from Historical & Geographical treatment)
```
41         – Great Britain
0          – relation symbol
73         – United States
=  382.0941073
```

3. Colonisation of Great Britain in India

```
=  325.3420954
325.3    –  Colonisation
.33–.39  –  Colonisation by specific countries
.09      –  Directions are given to relate by 09
41       –  Great Britain
=  325.3410954
```

4. Russian investment in India = 332.67347054

```
332.673 3  –  .6739 Investment originating in
                     specific continent and countries
332.673       Investment
```
(–3–9 for Geographical treatment)
```
–47        – Russian who is investing
0          – Relation digit
54         – India
=  332.67347054
```

Use of Geographical subdivision

–1 with Geographical subdivision

3–9

= –1 with –3–9

Notation 1 of Geographical subdivision can adjust the numbers of Geographical division –3–9.

1. If the number of a country/continent under –3–9 is added to Geographical division –1, there will be put 0 in between them.

e.g. Torrid Zone –13 of Asia –5
        (–1)   (–3–9)
        = 130.5   = 1305
        Rivers of India = 1693054

2. It is reverse to above serial 1 rule. If the notation of country is put first, the number of Geographical subdivison –1 and its subdivisions are added with 009 and the first digit of the subdivision of –1 ([1]3 rivers) is to be deleted before adding the number.

(a) Rivers of India
        1693   – Rivers
        009   – Relation digit/symbol
        54   – India
        = 540.091693

(b) Birds of forest of India
        54   – India
        598.291
        0   – Connecting symbol
        152   – Forest
        598.29152054 OR
        598.295400952

(c) Cattles of torrid zone of Asia
        636.2 –   Cattles
        (There is no direction for Geographical division)
        –009 to be added
        –13   Torrid zone
        –5   Asia
        = 636.20091305

Other examples:

1. Political parties of Algeria =
                324.265   324.2 Political parties
                              – 65   Algeria

2. Birds of Sahara desert = 598.2966
   598.29   – Birds (Geographical treatment of axes)
   –66   – Desert (Table 2)

3. Foreign policy of Holland = 327.492
   327   – Foreign policy
   –492   – Holland

4. International trade of Romania = 382.09498
   382 = International trade/commerce (foreign trade)
   [.09 add area notation 1–9 from table 2 to base
   number 382.09]
   498   – Romania

5. Trade between U.K. and Communist block
   382.09   – International trade
   382.09<u>41</u>   – U.K.
   382.094<u>1</u><u>0</u> – Relation digit
   382.09410<u>1717</u> Communist block

6. Cancer disease in Jordan = 616.9940095695
   618   – Cancer
   009   – add digit
   5695   – Jordan

7. Rail road transportation in Japan
   385.09 + –52 = 385.0952

8. Industrial libraries in communist countries
   027.69 + 09 + 1717 = 027.69091717

9. Congress party of India
   3242 + 54 + C = 324.254C

10. Interior decoration art in Thailand
    747.2 + [708].9 + –593 = 747.29593

11. French trade with Mexico
    382.09 + –44 + 0 + –72 = 382.0944072

12. Cultural treaty between India and China
    341.767 + [341]0266 + –54 + 0 + 51

13. Population movement from Bangladesh to India — its social implications

     304.8 + –54 + 0 + 5492 = 304.85405492

14. Elementary education in Indian villages

     372.9 + –1734 + 0 + –54 = 372.91734054

     372.9 + –54 + 009 + [1]734 = 372.954009734

15. Collection of treaties between India and Bangladesh on air transportation

     341.7567 + [341].0266 + –54 + 0 + –5492

     = 341756702665405492

16. Exchange rate between currencies of India and United Kingdom

     332.45609 + 54 + 0 + –41 = 332.4560954041.

9

Table – 3
Subdivisions of Individual Literature

- These are not used alone.
- These are added to base number for individual literatures identified by * under 810–890.
- Table 3 is followed and supplemented by table 3A which provides additional elements for building numbers within table 3.

Rules

1. Find the base number, that is designated or number column of the schedule 810–890.

   e.g. English language literature = 82
   Dutch language literature = 839.31

   For literary form of language of literature proceed to step 2, otherwise step 7.

2. Use table 3 to find the correct subdivision for the literary form.

   e.g. Poetry, Drama, Prose
   Add this number with base number.

   Examples:

   (a) English poetry   821
   (b) Dutch poetry   839.311

3. There is a period table with 810–890. If there is a period table, proceed to step 4. But if it cannot be used, class number is complete by insertion of a decimal points between third and fourth digit.

Example: 20th century drama in English by

New Zealand Authors – 828.993322
Cambodian poetry – 895.9391

Example:

Collection of contemporary
English language poetry by African authors

English (810–890)	82	(820)
Poetry (Table 3)	I	
of later 9th century (810–890)	914	(p. 1404)
Collection (Table 3)	080	
by Racial, ethnic, national groups (Table 3-A)	8	
Africans (Table 5)	96	(p. 411)

= 821.914080896

If title has no language

If "language of literature" term is not given in the title or the literature does not belong more than one language, then in both the cases the number will be taken from 801–809.

Use of standard subdivision

If title has a term related to standard subdivision –01 – 07, then it will be taken from 801–807.

e.g. Literary Awards   807.9

(800)   8   –   Literature
           079   –   Award

Rhetoric composition (Speech or writing)

If it is a Rhetoric composition, take from 800 or 808.1–7.

e.g.

(a) French Rhetoric

808.04   Rhetoric in specific language

(Class Rhetoric of specific kinds of composition regardless of languages in 808.06, <u>AND</u> preparation of manuscripts regardless of language in 808.02
$$= 808.04 \ \underline{41}$$

(b) Rhetoric of epic poetry
808.1 Rhetoric of poetry
<u>10</u>2–108 = [10]3 Epic (Table 3)
$$= 808.13.$$

It is a collection

If it is a collection, shown from the title of the book, then it will be classified in 808.8. If it is not a specific form of literature then classify it in 808.808–803. But if the literature has a specific form, classify it in 808.81 – 808.88.

Examples:

1. Collection of literature displaying idealism
$$= 808.8013$$
808.801 – 803 = Collection displaying specific features. (If direction is given to add 1–3 notations from table 3A to base number 808.80)
$$= 808.80 + 13.$$

2. Collection of 19th century poetry:
$$= 808.81034$$
808.81 collection of poetry
(There is direction index * divide like 808.81 – 808.88)
Under special table 01–05 is <u>Historical periods</u> which will be used leaving –090. = 19th century = 09034
$$= 808.81 + 0 + [090] \ 34 = 808.81034$$

There are specific forms of individual literature:

1. Poetry	5. Speeches
2. Drama	6. Letters
3. Fiction	7. Satire and humour
4. Essays	8. Miscellaneous writings

Notation for specific forms

1. Notations – 901–009 are used to indicate standard subdivision — collection, history, description, critical appraisal in the following manner:

– 001–007	Standard subdivision
– 008	Collection
– 009	History, description, critical appraisal

2. Notations 1–9. These are used to indicate specific periods as well as description, critical appraisal, biography, single and collected words of individual authors regardless of kinds of forms:

e.g.

Poetry of specific period 011–19

011–19	Poetry of specific period
021–29	Drama of specific period
031–39	Fiction of specific period

3. Specific kinds, media, scope etc. of specific form:

– 102–108	Specific kinds of poetry
– 202–205	Drama of specific kinds media, scope
– 301–308	Fiction of specific scope and types
– 501–506	Specific kinds of speeches
– 802–808	Specific kinds of miscellaneous writings.

Broad divisions on the basis of which each form of literature may be divided

1 – Poetry

– 1001–1007	Standard subdivision
– 1008	– Collection of poetry by more than one author from more than one period.
– 1009	– History, description, critical appraisal of poetry from more than one period.
– 102–108	Specific kinds of poetry.
– 11–19	Poetry of specific period.

Points to note. While using the notations in respective forms of literature enumerated from 2–8, ensure

1. That in all these forms 001–009 is designated as standard subdivisions. The instruction provided under it directs the classifier to add numbers following –100 in –1001–1009.

It means the specific concepts enumerated under –1 poetry or instructions given therein are commonly applicable to all the forms.

2. That the notations of kinds, scope, types etc. of these literary forms are enumerated under each specific form itself.

Steps used when form is 1 Poetry

Stage A – Write down the base number for the specific literature as provided under 810–890.

Stage B – Check if it is identified by * asterisk.

Stage C – Add to it notation for poetry 1 from table 3.

Stage D – If the work is displaying specific feature or element or theme or subject, then these may be added.

Stage E – Add notations from table 3–A as per instructions under –1008 and –1009.

Stage F – If time facet is needed, see instructions under 11–19.

Examples:

1. Collection of poetry in literature displaying idealism

808.1–808.88 Collection of specific forms (p. 1304)
= 808.8
1   Poetry (Table 3)
= 808.81
13   Idealism (Table 3A)
= 808.8013

2. Collection of short stories

808.83
[30]1 –   Short stories   (p. 394 J. 3)
= 808.8031

3. Collection of 19th century poetry

808.81   Collection of poetry
0   Connecting digit
34   19th century
=   808.81034

4. Collection of literature by Punjabis

808.89	Collection for and by specific kinds of persons (Standard subdivision)
0	Connecting digit
142	Punjabis (T5)
808.89<u>0</u>	
8	(Literature for or by special racial, ethnic, national group) (Table 3 p. 402)
[91]42	Punjabis

= 808.89<u>0</u>8142

5. History of 19th century literature

809	
809.01.–.05	Literature from specific period
09	(Standard subdivision p. 10)
[0901–0905]	Historical period
(Class in 09)	
09034	19th century

= 809.034

6. Research on Hindi poetry:

891.43	Hindi *
–1	Poetry (Table 3)
–[1]001–[1]007	Standard subdivision (T1)
(0072) (T1)	Notations from table 1
–0072	Research (Table 1) (page 8)

= 891.43   Hindi

= 891.4310072

7. Collection of Hindi poetry displaying idealism

Hindi	891.43	
Poetry	1	(Table 3) Add to 10080 from Table 3–A
Collection	[1]0080	
Idealism	13	(Table 3–A)

= 891.4310080913

8. History of literary criticism upto early 20th century

891.95   Criticism
.9501–.9509   Standard subdivision
–09042   – 1920 – 1930 (Table 1)
= 801.9509042.

Works by or about individual authors — Broad Guidelines

1. Literary work of an individual author is to be classified by language in which work is originally written, regardless of the country.

2. That such a work is to be classified with the form in which the individual author writes the literature.

3. If the works by an individual author covers two or more forms of literature, classify the work with the form with which the author is mainly identified.

4. That after form number, period number may be added.

5. That if the works of an individual author are neither limited to, nor identified by one specific form, then the works of the individual author may be classified in –8 Miscellaneous writings.

6. That the notations enumerated for specific features, specific kinds or types of specific forms of literature are not applicable to works of individual author.

7. That the base number always means the number for specific literature in which the individual author writes his literary works and as provided in schedules from 810–890.

8. That the main elements required for classifying literary works of an individual author are:

Language number: Provided in the schedules from 810-890

Form Number: 1–8 from Table 3

Period Number: From period take as under specific literature.

9. That the form of point of view of practical classification the works of individual author may be divided into:

(a) Works in one specific form

(b) Works regardless of form.

Example:

Reminiscences of a Greek author of early 20th century

889* – Modern Greek ⎤
32 – Period table ⎬ Schedule
1900–1945 ⎦

Table 3 – –8 Miscellaneous writings
Add to –8 the notation from period table for the specific literature.

Where there is no period table in the schedule

If there is no period table in the schedule in 810–890.

Table 3

–81–89 Miscellaneous writings of specific periods.

The last paragraph under this number directs the classifier that —

If there is no period table, classify quotations epigrams, anecdotes of all periods in –802; diaries, journals, reminiscences of all periods in –807; prose literature of all periods in –808.

Example:

Anecdotes in English by an Indian author of 18th century.

828 + 02 = 828.02
In 828 + –102 = In 808.102 when option used.
828.026.

More than one author (collected works)

In case of collected works of more than one author, ensure the following:

1. That this category covers collected works of more than one author writing in one specific language.

2. That such a work is to be classed with specific form in which the collected works is written.

3. That if such a work is neither limited nor identified by one specific form then it may be classed in –8 miscellaneous.

4. That such a work may be subdivided on the basis of specific periods, scopes, kinds or types of specific forms of literature.

5. That to classify such a work, subdivisions of two different tables are to be used. Table 3 + Table 3–A.

6. That from the point of view of practical classification the works by or about more than one author may be divided into:

(1) Collected works not restricted to one specific form.

(2) Collected works restricted to one specific form.

(1) Collected works not restricted to one specific form

For a literary work by or about more than one author not restricted to one specific form, the subdivisions required are:

–08	Collection
–09	History, description, critical appraisal
–08	Collection procedure to be used
–08	Collections
Add to	–08 the notation –01–09 from table 3–A.

Steps to be used

1. Write the base number for specific literature as provided in 810–890 identified.

2. Add to the above base number –08 from table 3.

3. Then add required notation from table 3–A.

4. If the required notation from table 3–A is from –01–09 specific period, then add only 0 after 080 from table 3–A *i.e.* 0800.

5. After this, add number from period table given for specific literature in the schedules under 810–890.

Example:

An anthology of Bengali literature

Base No.		Collection table 3
891.44	+	–08
	=	891.4408

Collections of Bengali literature dealing with library

Base Number	Collection Base No.	Table 3-A
891.44	–080	–2
(Bengali literature)	(Collection Number)	(Literary)

= 891.440802

Collection of 19th century Bengali literature

Base No.	Collection Base No.	Notation 01–09 from table 3–A	Period No.
891.44 +	–080 +	0 +	4

= 891.440800<u>04</u>

–09 History, description, critical appraisal procedure to be used

For practical purpose the notation –09 may be divided in the following number:

(a) by specific period

(b) by additional elements enumerated in table 3–A.

(a) **By specific period**

The provisions and the instructions to add –09 notation from period table are one and the same in both the editions. The instruction is given in the following manner:

–09001–09009 Literature from specific periods

Add to –0900 the notation from the period table for the specific literature in 810–890.

Steps to be taken

1. Write the base number for specific literature as provided in 810–890.

2. Add –0900 to the base number as is given for –09 in table 3.

3. Then add specific period number as provided in period table under the specific literature.

Example:

History and description of Marathi literature upto 1947.

Base No. –09 Base No.   Period No. as under 891.4

891.46   +   –0900 +   7

                    = 891.4609007

<u>A collection biography of Marathi authors upto 1947</u>

    = 891.4609007

(b) **By additional elements**

Table 3–A is enumerated. This subdivision may also be used through –09 to provide additional elements in specific literature. Following procedure is to be used to add notation from table 3–A through –09.

(i) Write the base number of the specific literature as provided in 810–890;

(ii) Add to base number –09 table 3 wherein the instruction under –091–099 literature displaying specific features – Add to –09 notation 1–9 from table 3–A.

(iii) Then add notation from table 3–A.

Example:

Critical appraisal of Sanskrit literature displaying romanticism

Base No.   Critical App. Table 3   Table 3–A

891.2   +   –09   – 145

        =   891.209145

Collected biography of Sanskrit literary authors dealing with the social themes.

Base No.   Biography table 3   Table 3–A

891.2   –09   +   –355

        = 891.209355.

History of Swedish Literature

839.7   Swedish

–09   Table 3 for History

= 839.709

Collected works restricted to one specific form

To classify works by or about more than one author written in one specific form *i.e.* in poetry and drama or fiction etc. three different combinations are provided. DDC permits to add to specific form the following:

A. First Combination

Specific form + –001–009 standard subdivisions, collections, history, description..... + Table 3–A. Additional notation for literature.

Or

B. Second Combination

Specific form + specific period + Table 3–A. Additional notation for literature.

Or

C. Third Combination

Specific form + specific scopes, kinds, types + Table 3. Additional notation for literature.

A. Work related to more than one period

Specific form + 001–009 standard subdivisions, collections, history description.... + Table 3–A — Additional notation for literature.

The procedure to add above notation is similar in edition 19 and 20.

The notation –001–009 standard subdivision, collection, history etc. are enumerated under –1 poetry *e.g.*

–1001	– 1007	Standard subdivision
Table 3—	– 1008	Collection
	– 1009	History

and under –1008 and –009 the instructions to add notation 1–9 from table 3–A is provided. Under all other forms 2–8 instruction is provided directing the classification to add numbers following 100 in –1001 –1009. In other words to add notation of table 3–A to forms 2–8 help of the instruction provided under –1008 and –1009 is required.

Practice steps

(a) Write the base number for specific literature from the schedule as is given in 810–890.

(b) To this add notation –001–009 standard subdivision, collection, history...from table 3.

(c) If the notation is –08 collection or –09 History.... Then follow the instructions given under:

–1008 and –1009 in Poetry as well as in different forms under the heading standard subdivisions (Table 3).

(d) Then add required notation from table 3–A.

Example:

Collection of Punjabi drama covering different periods displaying comedy.

Table 3

–2 Drama

–2001–2009 standard subdivision

Add –200 the numbers following –100 in –1001–1009

–1008 Collections

Add to –10080 notation 1–9 from table 3–A.

17 Comedy (Table 3–A)

Encyclopedia of Hindi Drama – 891.432003

Punjabi Language Base No.	Drama Base No.	Collection Base No.	Notation from Table 3–A
891.42	+ –200	+ –80	17

= 891.422008017

Encyclopedia of Hindi Poetry

891.43 Hindi literature

–1001.1007 (Table 3) for standard subdivision (Table 1)

–03 Encyclopedia

= 891.43 + –1003 = 891.431003

B. Work related to specific period

Specific form + specific period + Table 3–A

The necessary instructions to add specific period number and additional notation for literature is provided under each form *e.g.*

Table 3

–11–19 Poetry of specific periods

Add to –1 the notation from period table for the specific literature then to the result add the numbers following –10 in –1001 –1009.

Example:

Collection of 19th century Punjabi poetry displaying comedy.

Punjabi Language Base No.	Poetry Base No.	Period No. as under	Collection Base No.	Comedy table
891.42	+ –1	+ 4	+ 080	+ 17

= 891.421408017.

Practice steps

  (i) Write base number for specific literature from the schedules in 810–890.

 (ii) To this, add specific form number from table 3.

(iii) Then add number for specific period as provided for specific literature in 810-890.

(iv) If desired, then add numbers following –10 in –1001 –1009 and then add further instructions under –1008 and –1009.

Add <u>0</u> and to the result add further as instructed under 1–8 specific forms (features).

Examples:

Collections on 19th century Hindi poetry dealing with religious concepts:

Hindi Language Base No.	Poetry Table 3	Period No. as under 891.4
891.43	+ –1	+ 9

Then to the result add numbers following –10 in –1001 –1009. It means the required number would be –1008 collection....

Add to –10080 notations 1–9 from 3–A
Table 3–A   382 Religious concepts
i.e. [–10] 080 + 382
      = 891.4314080382.

If there is no period table for the specific literature, add nothing to the form and the class number upto form be treated as complete.

C. **Specific types, kinds and scope of forms**

Specific form + kinds, scope + Table 3–A.

There are readymade numbers. To these notations from table 3–A may be added as per instruction given under –1–8, specific form under which the instruction states 'add to notation for each term identified by * (asterisk)' as follows:

01–07   Standard subdivisions
08 Collection
            Add to –08 notation.... from Table 3–A.

Practice steps

(a) Write base number for specific literature from the schedules 810–890.

(b) Add to this number from table 3, enumerated number for kind, scope from the required form e.g. –102 dramatic poetry.

(c) If the term for kind etc. is identified by * then add –08 or –09.

(d) Then add notation from 3–A.

Example: Collection of Hindi short stories dealing with places.

Base No.	Form	Collection	Table 3–A
891.43	+ –301	+ –08	+ 32
	= 891.433010832		

Critical appraisal of Hindi dramatic poetry of 19th century — –102 Dramatic

Base No.		Form		Critical		Table 3–A		Period
Language		Kind		App.				
891.43	+	–102	+	.09	+	.0		4
		= 891.431020900̲4						

Literature in more than one language

Literature works dealing with literature in General or related to more than one language are to be classed under main class 800 literature itself or its subdivisions from 801–809. The class numbers 801–809 are divided into three main subdivisions.

801–807   Standard subdivisions.

808   Rhetoric and collections of literary texts from more than one literature.

809   History, description, critical appraisal of more than one literature.

801–807   Standard subdivisions.

801 standard subdivision on philosophy and theory has been further subdivided to cover specific concepts like value, influence, psychology, history, techniques and theory of literary criticism. The classifier should note that DDC has specifically instructed under 809 to 'class theory, technique, history of literary criticism' in 801.95 and not in 809. The class number 801.95 has been further subdivided on the basis of specific literary forms.

Example:

History of literary criticism upto early 20th century
801.95   Criticism
            Theory, technique, history
.9501–.9509 Standard subdivisions
.09042   1920–1930 (Table 1)
= 801.9509042.

808 Rhetoric and collections

Works on the art of speaking or writing in an impressive and effective style and collections of literary texts from more than one literature are subdivided in the following manner:

808.001–009 standard subdivisions of rhetoric standard subdivisions from table 1 are to be added with works on rhetoric using two zeros, *e.g.*

Smith W. Art of rhetoric in Alexandria: its theory and practices in ancient world.

808	Rhetoric and collections
.001–.009	Standard subdivisions of rhetoric
–01	Philosophy and theory (Table 1)

= 808.001.

808.02–.06 **General topics in Rhetoric**

This covers techniques of writing editorial, writing for publications and rhetoric in specific languages using notations of table 6 Languages, as well as subdivision from 808.1–808.7.

Example: Literature for learning Hindi Rhetoric

808	Rhetoric and collections
.04	Rhetoric is specific language
.43–.049	in other languages

Add to base number 808.04 notations 3–9 from table 6

–9143 Hindi (Table 6)

Base No.	Table 6
808.04 +	–91431

= 808.0491431.

Rhetoric for children

808.06	Rhetoric of specific kind of composition
.0668	Children's literature
.0681–.0687	Specific literary form

Add to base number 808.068 the numbers following 808 in 808.1–808.7.

808.1 Rhetoric of poetry

Base No.	Add number following 808
808.068	

808.1–.7 Rhetoric in specific literary forms are to be subdivided on the basis of the notations of table 3 and its supplementaries *e.g.*:

Art of writing drama for radio and television

808.2 Rhetoric of drama

Add to 808.2 numbers following
–20 in notation 202–205 from table 3
[–20]2 for radio and television
Base No.   Table 3
808.2   +   [–20]2
= 808.22

808.8 Collection from more than one literature

This is again subdivided on the basis of specific periods, specific features, specific forms and specific kinds of persons. For subdividing all these concepts the classifier is instructed to add historical periods from standard subdivisions and notations from table 3 and its supplementaries, *e.g.*

Collection of 20th century literature

808.8001–.8005 Collection from specific periods

Add to base numbers 808.800, the numbers following –090 in notation 0901–0905 from table 1.

Base No.   Periodical (Table 1)
808.800   +   –[.090]4
= 808.8004

Collection of literature in varied languages by Indians

808.9   Collections for and by specific kinds of persons

Add to base number 808.89 notation 8–9 from table 3–A.

Table 3 —   –8 literature for and by Racial,
                   ethnic.........

Add to –8 notation 08–33 from table 5

Table 5   –91411   Indian
Base No.   Table 3–A   Table 5
808.89 +   –8   +   –91411
= 808.89891411

809 History, description, critical appraisal of more than one literature

809.1–.7 Literature in specific forms.

Instead of adding notations of table 3 and its supplementaries directly to 809, the classifier is required to add number following 808.81–808.87, thereby saving unnecessary

repetition of enumeration and instruction under each form
e.g.:

Example:

History and description of western fiction

809.1–.7 Literature in specific forms

Add to base number 809 numbers following 808.8 in
808.81–808.81, *i.e.*

808.83   Collection of fiction

808.831–838   Specific scopes and types

Add to base number 808.83 the numbers following –30 in
301–308 from table 3.

[–30]874   Western fiction

Base No.   Nos. following   Table 3   No. following 30
 809   +   [80878]3   +   [–30]874
    = 809.83874.

Literature for and by specific kinds of persons

The various types of literature for and by specific kinds of
persons may be subdivided on the basis of notations from
table 3–A, table 5 and the class numbers of the schedules from
001–999.

Example:

Literature by Tibetans
809.889   Other
Add to base number 809.889
Numbers following –9 in notation 91–99 from table 5
–954   Tibetans

Base No.   Table 5   Nos. following 9
809.889   +   [–9]54
    = 809.88954

Appraisal of literary works in natural sciences

809.935   Literature emphasising subjects
    Add to base number 809.935
    Notation 001–999
500   Natural Science

Base No.   Add from 001–999
809.935   +   5 [00]
  = 809.955

Options

1. To give local emphasis and a shorter number other than American literature in English class it in 810 *e.g.* Hindi literature and class American literature in 820.

2. To give preferred treatment by placing before 810 through use of letter or other symbol, *e.g.* 8 HO Hindi literature.

Base number for this would be 8H.

3. Two different methods may be used to provide local emphasis where two or more countries share the same languages. These are:

(a) By using initial letters: For example, those counters which share English language may distinguish the English language literature by using initial letters of that particular country, *e.g.*:

Literature of England   E820
Literature of India   In 820
Literature of Scotland   S820

(b) Use of the special number designated for literature of those countries that are not preferred, *e.g.*

If the classifier does not want to use the above methods (options 1 to [a]), he may use the class number specially provided by DDC for literatures of those countries which are not preferred *e.g.*:

810   American Literature in English

819   American Literature in English not requiring local emphasis.

(a) Canada

(b) United States

(c) Mexico

4. If the classifier has used either of the above methods, in that case he has to use the period table also accordingly, *i.e.*

classifier has to use only that period table which is provided for that particular country.

For instance, under 820 literatures of English and Anglo-Saxon languages, the following period table are provided.

Period table for English

For African countries
For Asian countries
For Australia
For Great Britain
For New Zealand
For South Africa

Example:

Later 20th century drama in English by Indian authors:

First Method

        822 English Drama
        Period Table for Asian countries
        3 Later 20th century 1947 —

C.No.   in 822.3

Second method —

  828   English miscellaneous writings
  .99   English language literature not requiring local emphasis
.9935 * India

(*Add to base number as instructed under 810–890 through this instruction notations of table 3 may be used.)

–2 Drama

–21–29   Drama of specific periods
            Add to –2 the notation from the period table for the specific literature.

820   Literature of English
             Period table for English
             For Asian countries

3   Later 20th century 1947

Base No.   Drama   Period Table
828.9935 +   −2   +   3
= 828.993523

Practical problems

1. Paradise lost by John Milton (1604–1674) = 821.4
2. Biography of 19th century Gujarati poets – 891.4714
3. An anthology of old person literature – 891.5108
4. Complete works of Shakespeare with notes – 822.22 (T3A)
5. Technical writings in Russian language – 808.66609171
6. An art of story-telling – 808.543
7. Collection of German narrative poetry – 831.0308
8. Description of Italian essays of renaissance period – 854.209
9. Collection of English poetry
   82   English Literature
   −1008   Collection of poetry (Table 3)
   = 821.008
10. Collection of English drama
    82   English Literature Drama – 2
    [1]008 Collection of poetry
    = 822.008
11. Collection of English Essays
    82   –   English Literature
    4   –   Essays (T3)
    [1]008 –   Collection
    = 824.008
12. Collection of English Poetry dealing with seasons
    82   English Literature
    1008 (T3) for base No. 10080
    1–9 (3A)
    33 Times (3A)
    82 + 10080 + 33 = 821.008033

13. Collection of English drama displaying fantasy = 822.08015

14. History of Hebrew poetry – 892.41009

15. History of Hebrew fiction – 892.43009

16. Criticism of Chinese erotic poetry – 895.110093538

17. Evaluation of Chinese erotic drama – 895.120093538

18. Biography of French poets – 841.009

19. Collection of Swedish poetry of reformation period – 839.71208

20. Collection of French drama of classical period displaying naturalism – 842.408012

21. Critical appraisal of fairy tales in later 20th century Hindi fiction = 891.433709375

22. Collection of romantic Hindi drama for radio and television – 891.4320208145

23. Evaluation of English love stories by Bengalis – 823.0850989144

24. Hindi literature – 891.43

25. Hindi poetry – 891.431

26. Hindi poetry from 1920 to 1940 – 891.4316

27. Collection of English Romantic poetry – 821.0080145

28. History of lyric poetry – 809.14

29. Critical study of 20th century Spanish drama
    86 + 2 + 6 + [–10]09 = 862.609

30. Premchand — a critical study (born 1880)
    891.43 + –3 + 4 + [–10]09 = 891.433409

31. Realism in French drama
    84 + 2 [–1]009 + 12 = 842.00912

32. Collection of American lyric poetry
    81 + –104 + 08 = 811.0408

33. Russian fictions of 18th century
    891.7 + –3 + 2 = 89.732

34. Collection of drama for motion pictures
    808.82 + 0 + [–090]33 = 808.82033

35. Collection of essays on nature
    808.849 + 36 = 808.84936

36. Collection of literature displaying realism
    808.80 + 12 = 808.8012

37. Encyclopedia of Japanese literature
    895.6 + –03 = 895.603

38. All India English poets Association
    82 + –100 [6] + [–0] 60 + 54 = 826006054

39. Biography of Shakespeare
    822.33 + 1 – 822.33B

40. Romeo & Juliet of Shakespeare
    822.33U3 = 822.33U3

41. Collection of English literature of Indian author
    82 + –080 + 8 + –91411 = 820.80891411

42. History and criticism of literature by Indians
    809.8 [9] + 9 + –54 = 809.8954

43. Collection of Eastern Hindi Literature
    891.4908 = 891.4908

44. Russian short stories — a bibliography
    891.7 + –301 + –016 = 891.7301016

10

Table – 4
Subdivisions of Individual Languages

These notations are never used alone but may be used with base number for individual languages identified by * as explained under 420–490, *i.e.* English has number 42. Phonology (–15 in this table): 42.5.

Stages

1. Write the base number of the specific language as given in 420–490;

2. Verify if the language is identified by * (asterisk) or T (Dagger) —

If yes

3. Then add to the base number, the required notation from Table 4.

Example:

Grammatical sketch of Dard languages
491.499 Dard languages
          Examples – Kashmiri – 491.499

(As the language is not identified by *. The notation of table 4 cannot be added to it.)

Phonemic and morphemic frequencies in Hindi

491.43   Western Hindi languages * Hindi
          491.43 – Base number

–5 Structural systems (Grammar) of the standard form of the language.
(Classify here comprehensive works on morphology, syntax and phonology [Table 4])

Base No.		Table 4
491.43	+	–5
= 491.345		

–2 Etymology of the standard form of the language

–24 Foreign elements

Etymology means the science or investigation of the derivation and original significance of words. It covers the origin and development of linguistic form as shown by determining its basic elements, discovering its earlier known use, recording changes in its form and meaning.

Practice steps

1. Write base number of the specific language under study from 420-490.

2. Add to the base number notation – 24 (T.4).

3. Then add from table 6 the number for the language whose words are used in the above specific language.

Example:

Use of English words in Hindi Language

491.43   Western Hindi language * Hindi
491.43   Hindi (Base number)
–24   Foreign elements (T.4)
Add to –24 notation 1–9 from Table 6
–21   English (T6)

Base No.		Table–4		Table–6
491.43	+	–24		–21
= 491.432421				

Use of Urdu words in Hindi Language

491.43   Hindi
Add as instructed under 420–490
420–490   Specific language
Under each language identified by * add subdivision of

individual language notation of 01–86 from Table 4 to designated base number.

–24 Foreign element (Add language notation 1–9 from Table 6, 6 to 24)

9, 439 Urdu (T6) 491.43124 + 91434 = 491.432491434

–3 Dictionaries of the standard form of the language

A dictionary is a book containing the words of a language or the terms of a specific subject arranged alphabetically. It provides meaning of the words or terms, their etymology, pronunciation, etc.

–31 Specialised dictionaries (synonyms)

Such as

Dictionaries of abbreviations, acronyms, synonyms, autonyms, and homonyms....

Examples:

Webster's new dictionary of synonyms, springfield, Massachusetts, 1968

420 * English and Anglo-Saxon languages
Table 4 –3 Dictionaries.........
        –31 Specialised dictionaries

Base No.   Table 4
  42   +   –31
= 423.1

Dictionary of abbreviations and symbols

420 * English and Anglo-Saxon languages
Base Number English 42
Table –3 Dictionaries
       –31 Specialised dictionaries

Base No.   Table 4
42   +   –31
420 + 31 =   420.31

LANGUAGE DICTIONARIES

Subdivisions of Individual Language

1. This is special subdivision of language.

2. It is used like a General subdivision.

3. It lists:

   (a) Problems
   (b) aspects
   (c) tools.

4. Notations may be used/added to any item in 400 Language, not in any other class.

> – 01 – 02 Standard subdivision
>   (Notation from Table 1)
>
> – 03 Dictionary, Encyclopedia, concordance
>   (Class dictionaries of standard form of the language in – 3, Non-standard form in –7)
>   – 05 – 09 Standard Subdivisions
>   (Notation from table 1).

Example: <u>Portuguese grammar</u>

Portuguese Language	=	46 (Base number)
Grammar	=	465

Example: <u>A Dictionary of standard Czechoslovakian</u>

Czechoslovakian Language = 491.863

Rules

–1 Written and spoken codes of the standard form of the language.

–2 Etymology of the standard form of language.

–3 Dictionaries of the standard form of language.

–5 Structural system (Grammar) of the standard form of the language.

–7 Non-standard forms of the language.

–8 Standard usage of the language (Applied/person criptive) Linguistics.

Other Features

1. It is a very short table.

2. Main class + Language number form the base number.

3. Base number is enumerated.

4. The base number can be sharpened by the notations given in Table 4.

5. If required instructions to use table 6 are given.

6. In table 4 first the notations for standard subdivisions are given.

7. Except 0 3 all the standard subdivisions may be used in first instance.

8. –3 is allotted to dictionaries.

9. 1–5 are allocated to description and analysis of standard forms of the language.

10. Number 7 is used for Non-standard forms of the language like dialects, slangs etc.

11. No. 8 is used for standard usage of language.

Points to be noted:

1. Identify the base number.

2. Add number from table 4 directly to base number

English Number	=	42 + 5 = 425
Italian Phonology	=	45 + 15 = 451.5
Hindi dialects	=	491.43 + 8 = 491.438

Uses of Table 6 — Etymology (Foreign elements)

Bilingual dictionaries	24
	= 32-39
	= 824
One language for the people whose language is different	834
Reader for those whose native language is different	864

The class numbers for dictionaries of standard form of the languages in 420-480 have already been enumerated by DDC and so there is no need of using –3 from table 4 with these languages. However, languages enumerated under 490 have to take help of table 4 for this purpose.

Example:

Maharashtra Shabdkosh 4 Vols. 1932–37

491.46 * Marathi

    – 31   dictionaries of standard form of language (T4)

Base No.   T-4
491.46   –3
= 491.463

Bengali Shabdkosh	= 491.443
Hindi Grammar	= 491.435
Punctuation of Urdu words	= 491.439
Spelling of Russian words	= 491.781
English words in Hindi language	= 491.432421
Alphabets of Japanese language	= 495.611
Learn English through structured approach	= 428.2
How to translate in English from other language	= 428.02

– Dictionary of Hindi Abbreviations

491.43 Hindi (Add to base No. as instructed under 420–490)

420–490 specific language (under each language identified by * add subdivision of individual language notation 01–86 from Table 4 to designate base number)

3 Dictionaries

31 Specialised abbreviation = 491.43 + 31 = 491.4331

Dictionary of Urdu symbols = <u>491.43931.</u>

Bilingual Dictionaries

Bilingual dictionaries means a dictionary giving equivalent words in two different languages. It provides translation of words or terms of language into another, or explaining words or terms of the two languages in turn.

– English – Hindi dictionary.

DDC instructs to use number for one language from 420–490 and for another from table 6.

1. Class a bilingual dictionary with the language in which it will be more useful.

Example:

Comprehension English–Hindi dictionary.

420	English and Anglo-Saxon language base number for English <u>42</u>
–3	Dictionary (T4)
–32.39	Bilingual dictionaries Add to –3 notation 2–9 from table 6
–91431	Standard Hindi (Table 6)

Base No.	T-4	T6
42	+ –3	–91431

= 423.91431

– Marathi Language dictionary   491.463

2. If both languages are useful and classification of both the languages is necessary, classify with the language <u>coming later</u> in the sequence 420–490.

Example: Spanish–Latin dictionary

470	*Italic language Latin
47 –	Base number
–3	Dictionary (T4)
–32–39	Bilingual dictionaries

Add to –3 notation 2–9 from T6

–61	Spanish (T6)

Base No.	T4	T6
47	+ –3	–61

= 473.61

1. English French dictionary   443.21
2. French Russian dictionary   491.7347
3. Rughuvira's English Hindi Dictionary   423.91431
4. Dictionary of Physics   530.03 = 530.3
5. Dictionary of Political Science   320.03 = 320.3
6. French and German Dictionary   443.31
   (32–39 Bilingual [Add language notation
   2–9 from Table 6 to –3]
   31 German Table 6 to –3)
   31 German (T6)
   44 + 3 + 31 = 443.31

7. Punctuation marks in Russian language 491.73
   (420–490) specific language
   1 Punctuation (T4)

8. Malayalam Alphabets – 494.81211

Subject Dictionaries

It is confined to specific subject or several related subjects.

Subject dictionary is to be classed in the subject which it covers and the notation –03 dictionary is to be added to it from Table 1 standard subdivision.

Example:

1. Concise Dictionary of Physics and related terms

530	Physics
–01–.09	Standard subdivision
–03	Dictionaries, Encyclopedias, concordance

Base No.	T1
530	+ –03
= 530.03	

– Again subdivision by language of dictionary

– 03   Dictionary

–032–039 by language

Add 'languages' notation 2–9 from table 6 to base number –03

–21   English (T6)
     = 530.0321

Dictionary of Textile   –   677.003

–7 Historical and Geographical variations

The notation –7 is used to indicate the historical, geographical and modern non-graphical variations among the standard form of languages.

Therefore all the subdivisions enumerated from –1 to –5 and –8 of this table are also to be classed under –7 when these indicate to historical, geographical and modern non-geographical variations.

Sometimes one language is mixed with other language and distorted and twisted or modified in such a way that it requires a distinct style and way of speaking with altogether different meaning and grammatical characteristics.

Such language becomes a language of a particular area or region where it is so spoken. –7 is used to indicate some of such individual languages in 420–490.

Example:

1. A study of dialects of Bari

   457   Historical and Geographical variations

   .1–.7   Geographical variations in continental Italy

Add to 547 the numbers following

45 in notation 451–457 from table 2

Table 3   – 45751 Bari province

               Class here Bari

Base No.	No. following –45 (T2)
457	[–45]751
= 457.751	

2. Grammatical characteristics of the dialects of Eastern Siberia

   481.7   Russian

   .774–.779   Geographical variations

   Add to 491.77 notation 4–9 from Table 2

–575   Eastern Siberia (T.2)

Base No.	Table 2
491.77 =	–575
= 491.77575	

–8 Applied linguistics

There are following elements of linguistic *i.e.* meaning, spelling, pronunciation, grammar etc. Their use, study and learning is enumerated under –8.

Example:

1. Translating from English into Hindi

Translating	Table 4
To base number	Translating (Table 6)
491.43 +	–802
= 491.43802	

2. Learning Russian for those who know English language —

491.7 + 824 + 21 = 491.782421

Learning language

–82–86 These numbers are provided to classify the aids, readers, texts, which help in learning, or increasing proficiency of poor readers or to practice in reading a language to those —

(a) whose native language is different,

(b) native speakers who are learning the acceptable patterns of their language.

Examples:

1. Learning Russian for those who know English language

491.7	East Slovic language * Russian
491.7	Base number for Russian
–82	Structural approach to express in (T4)
–824	For those whose native language is different Add to –824 notation from T6
–21	English (T.6)
	= 491.7.78282421

2. French language proficiency reader

Base No.		Table 4
44	+	–842
= 448.42		

3. <u>Medical Science reader</u>

Base No.		Table 1
61	+	.14
= 611.4		

Three or more languages

The book dealing with comparison with three or more languages would be classed on the basis of the following rules:

1. Classify a comparison of Swedish, Danish and German Grammar = 430.

2. If there is no number that will contain all the languages than class such a work in 410.

Example:

Comparison of Russian Danish and German Grammar
= 415

3. Classify a comparison of two languages with the language requiring local emphasis (Language which is less common in a library)

Example:

Comparison of Sanskrit and Russian alphabets

= 491.711 (in India)

If no emphasis is required, class the work with the language covering later in Table 6.

4. Classify a language of a specific discipline or subject with the discipline or subject using notation 014 from table 1.

Example:

Terminology used in library and Information Science
= 020.14

Options

1. If emphasis is given to local language, classify in 410, add to base number 41 as instructed in 420–490.

Example:

    41   Hindi language
    413   Hindi language dictionary

2. To give local emphasis and a shorter number to a specific language, place it first by use of a letter or other symbol.

Example:

4 HO Hindi language

Base No. 4H
Add notation
from table 4.3
    = Hindi language dictionary

The place of this number would be proceeding to 420.
    i.e. 410 or 4HO or 491.43

Example:

1. Old Portuguese — 469.701
2. Dictionary of French Homonyms — 443.1
3. Arabic Russian dictionary — 492.739171
4. Works on Indian Euro. Language — 410
5. Comparative study of Hebrew, Arabic and modern Arabic language — 492
6. French, German and Russian dictionary — 413
7. Chinese Grammar — 495.15
8. Malyalam alphabets — 494.81211
9. Latin words in English language — 422.471
10. German Phonology — 431.45
11. French reader — 448.6
12. Webster's English dictionary — 423
13. Translation of Hindi into English — 491.43802
14. Punctuation marks in Russian Language — 491.71
15. Persian words in Urdu — 91.439249155
16. French abbreviations — 441

11

Table – 5
Racial, Ethnic, National Groups

1. This notation is used in the same way as the language notation, but to indicate the people.

2. These notations are never used above, but may be used as required.

3. These notations are used (either directly when so noted or through the interposition of "Standard Subdivisions" notation <u>089</u> from table 1) with any number from the schedule, *e.g.* ethno psychology = (155.84)

    ethno psychology of the Japanese (–956 in this table)

    <u>Ceramic arts</u>   = 738

        Of Jews = –924

        = 738

    Base Number + Standard subdivision + People Number
    (Class No.)   T.I. Base Number
                089
    738 + 089 = 934 = 738.089924

4. Except where the schedule instructs otherwise, and unless it is redundant, add 0 to the number from this table and to the result add "AREAS" notation 1–9 from table 2.

Examples:

    1. Germans in Brazil
          Germans + Brazil

2. Germans in Germany — 31 (Table 5)
3. Slave racial psychology —

Ethno psychology	= 155.8
Slave	4918
	= 155.84918
For language	– 089
For National ethnic	– 09

4. Psychology of Dravidians —

Psychology	– 155.84
Dravadians	– 948

5. World history of Jews — 909.04 + 909.4924
6. Social Study of Indians — 305.8 + 91421
   = 305.891411
7. Folk songs of Indian Gypsies — 784.76 + 91497
   = 784.7691497
8. Chinese Cookery = 641.592 + 951 = 641.592951
9. Education for Tibetians — 371.97 + 954 = 371.97954
10. Religion of Iranians (Mithraicism) — 29 + 915
    = 299.15
11. Religion of Bantus — 299.68 + 3 = 299.683
12. Psychology of Bengalis — 155.84 + 9144 = 155.849144
13. Poetry of Tamils — 738.2 + 089 + 948 = 738.2089948

Rule — All the notations from Table 5 can be used, even without any instructions, when required through the standard subdivisions number 089 from Table 1.

There is no separate number of Tamils. The Number of Dravadians will be used for Tamils.

Examples:

1. Marriage customs of Dravadians
   392.5 + 09 + 174 + 948 = 392.509174948
2. Collection of French Literature for Canadians of French origins
   84 + 08 + 0 + 8 + 114 = 840.808114

Table 5 provides —

1. Basic races – Negro race
2. Ethnic group – Sinhalese
3. National group of Indians or Japanese etc.

All divisions in Tables 5, 6 are similar to divisions based on languages and having the same sequence as is provided in 420–490 specific languages.

However Table 5 is necessary because —

(a) It refers to the group of people.

(b) The group of people may speak common language, yet may belong to different ethnic or cultural groups or nationality.

There are two specific orders in Table 5 —

1. **Citation order**
   (a) Ethnic group
   (b) Nationality
   (c) Basic races

2. **Order of precedence**

If document deals with any two or all three categories, then apply following rules:

(a) Minority Ethnic group *vis-à-vis* Nationality

Priority to Ethnic group

Example: Canadian citizens who are ethnic Japanese

```
–956   Japanese
  –0   Connecting symbol
 –71   Canada (T2)
     = 956071
```

(b) Ethnic group which is a citizen of a particular country moves to another country:

Example: Canadian citizens who are ethnic Japanese move to United States:

```
–956   Japanese (T5)
  –0   Connecting symbol
 –73   United States (T2)
```

(c) Among two national groups choose the former or ancestral national group.

Example: People of Japan who have become citizens of United States:

−956   Japanese (T5)
− 0   Connecting symbol
−73   USA (T2)
= 956073

Examples:

1. Cultural ethnology of North American native race

      572.8 +   −97   = 572.897

2. Social status of Tibetans

      305.8 +   −954 = 305.8954

Use of Table 5 through notation −089 (T.1)

If table 5 is used freely through standard subdivisions −089 from all class numbers of schedule where no instructions are given to add nation from Table 5.

Steps —

1. Write the base number for a specific subject from the schedules for which table 5 is required.

Remove 0 or zeros if the class number ends with zero.

2. Verify if instruction for the use of standard subdivisions is provided

If yes —

Then add zero as per instruction to −089 before adding it to the base number,

If not —

Then add directly.

3. Then add notations from table 5 as per instruction given under standard subdivision notation −089 racial, ethnic, national group.

Example:

Faith on astrological symbolism among Indians

133.5   Astrological symbolism

–089   Racial, ethnic, national groups (T1)
Add to base number –089 notation 03–99 from table 5
     = 91411   Indian (T5)
     = 133.508991411

Psychology of Mongolects

155.8   Ethno psychology
  .84   Special racial, ethnic groups
  035   (T5)
     = 155.84035

Folkways of Tibetans

390   Folkways
Use 390.001 – 390.009 for standard subdivision
–089   Racial, ethnic (Table 1)
–954   Tibetans (T5)
     = 390.0089954

Use with area notations

1. Connect through '0' as connecting symbol subject +
T5 + 0 + T2

Examples:

1. Psychology of Indians living in Kuwait
155.8   Ethno psychology and National psychology
  .84   Special racial, ethnic groups
Add to base number 155.84 notation 01–99 from Table 5.
–91411   Indian (T5)
–5367   Kuwait (T2)
     = 155.849141105367

2. Popularity of Punjabi Cookery in USA
641.592   Ethnic Cookery

Add to base number 641.592 notation –03–99 from
table 5.
–9142   Punjabis (T5)

Add 0 then add notation 1–9 from T2
–73   USA
     = 641.592914273

3. Education of women in religions where
   Anglo-Indians predominate

376   Education for women

376.9   Historical, geographical

Add to base number 376.9 notation – from table 2

–174   Region where specific racial, ethnic, national
          group predominates

Add to base number –174 notation –03–09 from Table 5 (T2)

–91411   Indians

Including Anglo-Indians (T5)

= 376.917491411.

Collections of literature by Indians

808.89   Collection for or by specific kinds of persons

Add to base number 808.89 notation –8–9 from table 3–A

–8 Literature for and by (T3–A)

–91411   Indians (T5)

= 808.89891411

Examples:

1. Punjabi folk songs   – 784.769142
2. Social study of Indians living in
   England   – 305.891411042
3. South Asian races   – 572.8914
4. World history of Afro-Americans   – 909.0496073
5. Biographies of French   – 920.009241
6. Causes of crimes in areas where gypsies
   predominate   – 364.917491497
7. Burmese Non-dominant aggregates – 305.8958
8. Gypsy Music   – 781.7291497
9. Education of Iranians in India – 371.97915054
10. Dravadian races — a biological study – 572.8948
11. Civilization among North Americans – 909.041
12. Labour strikes in the area where Sudanese
    predominate   – 331.8929174927624

13. History of Jews in Europe   – 940.04924
14. Manual of husband wife relationship
    for Americans   – 306.870913
15. Wedding and Marriage
    Customs among Indo-Aryans   – 392.5089914

12

Table – 6
Languages

These notations are not used alone but may be used with those numbers from the schedules and other tables to which the classifier is instructed to add "Languages" notation.

It belongs to specific languages number under 420–490 and 810–890 in the schedule. It involves the following:

1. Use of table 6 through instructions provided in specific subjects, discipline in the schedule.

2. Use of table 6 through instructions provided in notations in other table.

The notations of Table 6 may be added to only those class numbers where necessary instructions in this regard are given.

Example:

Gen. Encyclopedia written in Dutch language
030	General Encyclopedia work
03	In other Germanic languages

Add to base number 03 notation 2–9 from table 6
–3931	Dutch (T6)
=033.931	

Tamil folktales from Tamil speaking areas of the world

398.2	Folk literature
.204	By language
	– Add to base number 398.204 notation 1–9 from Table 6.

Class tables of specific language where that language predominates in 398.209.

Base No.   T6
398.20<u>494811</u> (T6)

Egyptian language
493   New Semetic Afro-Asian language
            Add to 493 the numbers following –93 in
            notation 931–937 from table 6.

–931   Egyptians (T6)

Base No.   Table 6 nos. following 93
493   [–93]1
= 493.1

Table – 1: Standard Subdivisions

Library & Information Sc. Glossary in Hindi

020   Lib. & Inf. Sc.
–03   Dictionaries
–932–039   By language
            Add language notation 2–9 from Table 6
            base number –03
–91431   Hindi (T6)
   =020.391431

Table – 2: Area

The notation of table 6 and table 2 may be added —

(a) Through instructions given in schedule

(b) Through area notation –175

(a) **Through Instruction in Schedule**

Tamil speaking people in Asia
   305.7 Language groups
Add to base number 305.7 notation 1–9 from Table 6.
Then add 0

And to the result add notation 1–9 (T2)
–94811   Tamil (T6)
–5   Asia

$$= 305.7 + 94811 + 0 + 5$$
$$= 305.79481105$$

(b) **Through Area**

As the area notation may be used through the notation –09 of standard subdivision T.1, classifier may use autonomy to use notation of table 2 through –175 as and when necessary.

Example:

Psychology of school children of areas where Maithili language predominates.

155.4   Child psychology
.424   Children six to eleven
–090   Treatment of area, regions – (SS T1)
       in 11–19 from Table 2.
–175   Regions where specific languages predominate (T2)

Add to base number –175 notation 1–9 from table 6.

   –91454   Maithili (T6)

Base No.	SS (T1)	No. following–1 (Table 2)	Table 6
155.424 +	–091	[–1]75 +	–91454

$$= 155.4240917591454$$

Through Table – 4 — Subdivisions for individual languages.

T.4 is for individual languages for main class 400 from 420–490.

T6 also enumerates similar languages in 420–490.

Therefore, notation of Table 6 are used with Table 4 only when the specific subject requires two different languages simultaneously.

Hence use —

(1) One language from schedule

(2) Another from table 6 through T.4.

Example:

Modern Greek reader for English speaking people
489.3   Modern Greek

–86   Readers (T4)

–864   For those whose native language is different

Add to –864 notation 2–9 from table 6

–21 English (T6)

Base No.	Table 4		Table 6
489.3	+ –864	+	–21
= 489.386421			

Examples:

1. Voting behaviour of areas where Urdu language predominates = 324.917591439

2. Bible in Hindi 220.591431

3. Serial publications in Urdu language 059.91439

4. French rhetoric through critical readings = 808.04417

5. Bengali proverbs 398.99144

6. Social status of German speaking people in U.S.A. = 305.731073

7. Collection of Essays in Hindi – 089.91431

8. Indonesian language 499.22

9. Translation of Talmudic literature in French = 296.120541

10. Whitaker's Almanac 032.02

11. Translation of Bible in Chinese = 2205951

12. Teaching of English in Elementary schools = 372.6521

13. Gen. Encyclopedia in Spanish language = 036.1

14. Gen. Serial publication in Hindi language = 059.91431

15. Translation of Koran in Hindi language = 297.122591431

13

Table – 7
Group of Persons

These notations are not used alone, but may be used as required (either directly when so noted or through the interposition of standard subdivisions, notation 088 from table 1) with any appropriate number from the schedules.

The notations and concepts enumerated in Table 7 have been based on enumeration of main classes of the schedules.

Subject specialists = 1–9 to main class 100–900

e.g.:

−1 Persons occupied with philosophy, psychology
−2 Persons occupied with religion
−3 Persons occupied with social sciences
−4 Persons occupied with linguistics.

Rules

Table 7 may be added to the class number of specific subjects of schedules.

(a) Through the instructions under specific subjects

(b) Through Table 1 standard subdivisions – 024 and 088.

Through instructions

Class numbers of schedule needs additional elements as enumerated in Table 7. DDC has directed to use notation of T 7 through instructions in the class numbers.

Steps

    1. Write the base number as instructed.

    2. Add to it required number from table 7.

    Examples:

    1. Ethics of Hotel and Motel (The hotel having car parking with the rooms for traveler) keepers

    174.9   Other profession and occupations

    Add to base number 174.9 notation –09–99 from table 7
        –647   Hotel and Motel Keeper (T7)
               = 174.9647.

    2. Reading and use of other information media by school children:

Base No.		Table 7
028.53	+	[–05]44
= 028.5344		

    Use of T.7 through T.1 standard subdivisions.

    The classifier may also use notations of Table 7 through Table 1. Standard subdivision –024 and –088 with all such specific subjects wherein no instruction is available for adding notations of Table 7.

Steps

    1. Write the base number for specific subject with which the notations of Table 7 are required to be used, *i.e.* remove zero or zeros if the class number ends with zero or zeros.

    2. Verify if the instruction for the use of standard subdivisions is provided.

    3. If yes, then add zeros as directed to –024 and 088 before adding the number to the class number of specific subjects, otherwise add directly.

    4. Then add notation from Table 7 as per instructions given under –024 and –088.

    024 Works for specific type of users

    Examples:

    1. Works on food and foodstuffs for old persons.

641.3   Food
–024   Works for specific types of users (T1) add to base
          number –024 notation 03–99 from table 7
0565   Late adulthood (T7)

Base No.   T1   As per Instru.   T7
  641.3   +   –024   +   0024   +   –0565
    = 641.300240565

2. Works on manufacture of textile and clothing for public entertainers

677 Textiles

Classify here comprehensive works on manufacture of textiles and clothing.
–024   Works for .... (Table 1)
–791   Public performances (Table 7)

Base No.   Table 1   As per Instru.   Table 7
  677   +   –024   +   –0024   +   –791
    = 677.0024791

–88 **Specific kinds of persons**

1. Under the notation –088 treatment among group of specific kinds of persons, the add instruction was used to add notation –04–99 from table 7 and there was no enumeration under –88.

2. All the 26 subdivisions of –06 have been enumerated under –06 in Table 7.

3. Those could be used through –088.

Example:

Correspondence school and courses for farmers

Base No.   Table 1   Table 7
374.4   +   –088   +   –631
    = 374.4088631

Use of Table 7 with Table 2 Area

In table 2 the notation –176 has been used to subdivide such areas as are dominated by people of specific religion.

For this purpose the notation of Table 7 enumerated under –29 with other religions, has been used and specific instruction to add notation from Table 7 is given under –176 Regions where specific religions predominate.

For areas predominated by Christian religion readymade class numbers are enumerated.

Example:

Factors affecting social behaviour in areas where Bahai faith predominates.

Base No.		Table 1		Table 2		Table 7
304	+	–09	+	–176	+	–2979

= 303.20917679

Table 3-A (individual literature) and Table 7.

Table 3–A enumerates additional elements for individual literatures enumerated under 810–890 in the schedule. In this table under the notation –92 for and by persons of specific classes, the instructions are provided through which the group of persons enumerated in Table 7 may be used with individual literatures, to indicate the specific group of persons for whom, by whom the literature is written. The added instruction is provided under –09204 –9279 and –929.

Example: **A collection of English fiction by lawyers**

Base No.		Table 3		Table 3–A	Table 7
82	+	–30088	+	–92	–344

= 823.008892344.

A Collection of Literature of Historians

Base No.		Table 3–A		Table 7
808.89	+	–92	+	–97

= 808.899297.

Examples:

1. Books on gardening for women – 635.024042
2. Ethics of food technology – 174.9664
3. Collection of literature for social workers – 908.89923362
4. Collection of literature for philosophies – 808.899211

5. Bibliographies of works by
   women authors   – 013.042

6. Customs of Muslims   – 390.42971

7. Bibliographies of works of
   librarians   – 013.092
   (013 + –092)

8. Collection of literature by Sikhs   – 808.89922946
   (808.89 + 92 + –2946)

9. Customs of languages   – 390.4344
   (390.4 + –344)

10. Costumes of nurses   – 391.04613
    (391.0 + [390].4 + –613)

11. Mathematics for engineers   – 510.2462
    (51[0] + –024 + –62)

12. Guide to intra family relationship
    for married persons   – 306.870880655
    (306.87 + –088 + –655)

13. Collections of Hindi literature
    by Parsees   – 891.4388092295
    (891.43 + –080 + 92 + –295)

14. Ethics of politicians   – 174.9329
    (174.9 + –329) or
    320.017

15. Ethics of statesmen   – 174.932
    (174.9 + –32)

16. Costumes of Military personnel   – 391.04355
    (391.0 + [390]4 + –355)

17. Calculus for management scientists – 515.02465
    (515 + –024 + –65)

18. General encyclopedia in Spanish language
    03   General Encyclopedia works
    –32–039 By Language

Add 'Languages' notation 2–9 from table 6 to base number –03.

= 036.1

19. Rajasthani Proverbs
398.9   Proverbs
Add notations from T.6. Rajasthani
91479
= 398.991479

20. Translation of Koran in Hindi language:

297.1225   Koran Translation
Add notation from T.6.
Hindi Language 91431
= 297.122591431

21. General collection of Essays in Marathi language

080   General Collection
081–089 in specific languages
089   Other languages
Add Languages notation 2–9 from table 6 to base number 089.
= 9146
= 089.9146

Kadambini, a Hindi Magazine

(p. 38)   050   General serial publications
059   in other languages

Add "Languages" notation 2–9 from table 6 : ba: number 059.
–91431   Hindi
= 059.91431

Tamil Encyclopedia

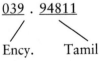

039 . 94811

Ency.   Tamil

Education of women in Urdu speaking areas of the world —

376   Education for women

Add 'areas' notation 1–9 from table 2 to base number 376.9

37.9   Education of women in areas

175   Regions where specific language predominates

Add 'Languages' notation 1–9 from table 6 to base number 175

= 1439 Urdu

= 376.917591439.

14

Generalia 000–009

1. Class of general nature.
2. Class though specific but general in nature
   (Lib. Sc., journalism, newspapers)

000	Generalia
010	Bibliography
020	Lib. & Inf. Sc.
030	General Encyclopedia works
040	
050	General serial publications
060	General org. & museumology
070	journalism, publishing, newspapers
080	General collection
090	MSS and book rarities

Examples:

1. Archaeologists 013.89 + 93 (Table 7) = 013.893
2. Bibliography of French Govt. Publications

Bibliography	015
France	44
(from table 2) add	0
Govt. publications	.53

   = 015.44053
3. Bibliography of serial publications on philosophy
   520.16 (016 from table 1)
4. Bengali Language collections

General collection   080
In other languages   089
(Add languages' notation 2–9 from table to base number 089)
Bengali   – 9144 (Table 6)
              = 089.9144

5. Cooperative Cataloguing   025.35
6. College Library Building   022.317
7. Library building in 1970   022.33047
8. Adm. of map collection in a map library 025.176
9. Acqisition of material in Social Sciences 025.273
10. Cat., Class-indexing of maps   025.346
11. Subject heading in Science   025.495
12. Circulation Services   025.6
13. Library of Congress   027.573
14. French Language encyclopedia   034.1
15. French Language Serial publications   054.1
16. New York Times   071.11
17. Universe of Kowledge, How classified   001.012
18. Research Methods in general   001.42
19. A world book Encyclopedia   031
20. Selection of Academic libraries   025.21877
21. Library Cooperation in India   021.640954
22. Public Libraries in Rajasthan   027.4544
23. Indexing of Maps   025.346

15

600 – Technology
(Applied Science)

600–609	– Standard subdivisions
603	– General Technology
610–619	– Medical Sciences
610	– Medical organizations, personnel, study and teaching, nursing practice.
611	– Human Anatomy, cytology, Tissue biology
612	– Human Physiology (Bio-Physics and Bio-Chemistry)
613	– Personal hygiene by sex and age group. Industrial and Military hygiene, physical fitness, addictions, birth control.
614	– Public health personnel, certification and registration of personnel, adultration, drugs, and food, and control of disease.
615	– Pharmacology and Therapeutics.
616	– Courses, effect, diagnosis, treatment and disease, medical microbiology, psychosomatics medicine.
616.1–618.8	– Disease of various systems — respiratory, digestive, blood forming, hymphatic and endocrine systems.

616.9	–	Fever, bacterial and viral diseases, parasitic diseases, allergies, cancer.
617	–	General Surgery
618	–	Gynaecology, pediatrics, geriatrics
619	–	Experimental medicine

1. Drug treatment of round worms in Animals

636.089	–	Veterinary Science
[61]6.965	–	Disease due to round worm (Nematoda)
061	–	Drug treatment (Spl. Aux.)

2. A study of inherited diseases among children

   618.92   –   Pediatrics
   .92001 - .92009 General aspects
      (Add notation 01–09 under 616.1–616.9
      to base number 618.920)
   [0]42 Inherited disease (Spl. Auxiliary)
   = 618.920042

3. Domestic Medicines used in common cold

   616.205   – Common cold (Coryze, Rhinitis)
   024   – Domestic medicine (Spl. Auxiliary)
   = 616.205024

4. Treatment of lung diseases by Vitamins and dictotherapy

   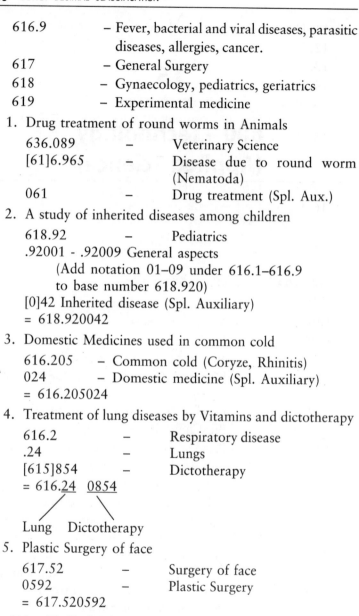

616.2	–	Respiratory disease
.24	–	Lungs
[615]854	–	Dictotherapy

   = 616.<u>24</u> <u>0854</u>

   Lung   Dictotherapy

5. Plastic Surgery of face

617.52	–	Surgery of face
0592	–	Plastic Surgery

   = 617.520592

610 – Medical Science

0   Medical org., Medical personnel, study & teaching and nursing practice.

11. Human anatomy, cytology, tissue biology
12. Human physiology
13. General health personnel, hygiene
14. Public health personnel, certification and registration and contamination of drugs and food including adultration and contamination of drugs and food.
15. Pharmacology and therapeutics — Drugs and group of drugs (synthetic, vegetable, animal), practical pharmacy and therapeutics (*i.e.* Homeopathy, osteopathy, chiropractic) and methods of medication.
16. Causes, effects, diagnoses, prognoses, treatment of disease, systems.
17. Surgery and related topics
18. Crynecology, obstetrics, pediatrics
19. Experimental medicine

Examples:

1. Drug treatment of round worms in animals

   Animals (Vet. Sc.) + round worms + treatment + Drug
   Veterinary Sciences   636.089
   (Add base number 636.089 the numbers following 61 in 610–619)
   Disease due to round worms (Nemotoda) [61]6.965
   Drug Therapy (Treatment) 061 (in 618.1–618.8)
       = 636.0896965061.

2. Parasitic skin disease among domesticated cats

   Cats
   General principles   .801–.808
   (Add to base number 636.80 the numbers following 636.0 in 636.01 – 636.08)
   Veterinary Sciences   –   636.089
   (Add to base number [636].089 the number following 61 in 610–619)
   Parasitic skin diseases   [61]6.57
   = 36.8089657.

3. Chemical diagnosis of skin ulcer in dogs

    Dogs   636.7
    General principle   .701–.708
    (Add to base number 636.70 the number following 636.0 in 636.01 – 636.08

    Veterinary Sciences   [636].089 (Veterinary medicine)
    (Add to base number 636.089 the numbers following 61 in 610 – 619)

    Skin Ulcerations   [61]6.545
    Pathology (Spl. Auxiliary)   07 (Spl. Auxiliaries 617)
    (Add to 07 the numbers following 616.07 in 616.071 – 616.079)

    Chemical diagnosis   [616.07]56
    636.708965450756.

4. Plastic surgery of face   617.520592

    Face   617.52
    Plastic surgery (spl. Auxiliary) 0592
    = 617.520592.

    Diseases in the tropics   614.4223
    Biography of Psychiatrists   616.890092
    Heart disease   614.5912
    Acupuncture   615.892
    Diagnosis of brain diseases 616.80475
    Cancer of hearts   616.99412.

16

800 – Literature

This class is used for —

(a) Works of literature

(b) Works about literature

(c) Literacy form includes —

(i)	Poetry
(ii)	Drama
(iii)	Fiction
(iv)	Essays
(v)	Speeches
(vi)	Letters
(vii)	Satire
(viii)	Humour
(ix)	Quotations
(x)	Epigrams

SCHEDULE

800 – General directions, table of precedence to follow for works of two or more literary forms.

Three main options

1. To class the literature in division 810.

2. To place specific literature to be emphasized before 810 by using a letter symbol.

3. In case where two or more countries have the same language, is either to use initial letters to identify separate

countries or to use the special number designated for literatures of those countries which are not preferred.

801 – Philosophy and theory of literature subsections —
  (a) Value
  (b) Influence
  (c) Effect of literature —
      Psychology, esthetics, criticism

801.95 Criticism

801.951–801.957 Criticism of specific literary form

802–807 (804 unassigned) — standard subdivisions

808 – rhetoric, collections of literature
  (a) Authorship
  (b) Editorial technique
  (c) Composition in various languages
  (d) Type of literature:
      (i) Professional
      (ii) Technical
      (iii) Childrens

808.1–808.7 – Covers rhetoric for specific forms of literature — Poetry, drama, fiction, essays, speeches, letters, satire and humour.

808.8 – Collection from specific period and special quality, specific theme and subjects (*e.g.* law, places, time, life cycles, philosophical concepts).

808.88 – Specific forms of literature on misc. topics.

809 – History, description, criticism.

809.1–809.7 – Literature in specific forms, and specific kind of persons (Age, group, sex, occupation).

809.9 – Specific features, qualities or elements.

810–890 – Literature of specific language.

Two principles

1. A work of literature is classed in the language in which originally written.

Example: Work in English translated from French, is to be classified in French literature.

2. A work of literature written in a dialect of a basic languages is classed with the basic language.

Example: A work written in Cockney — a dialect used in London (to be classified in Eng. Literature).

810	– American literature written in English:
	– Spl. provision has been made for English language literature of the Western Hemisphere and Hawaii. Instruction allow the literatures of specific countries to be distinguished by the use of letters before the DDC numbers.

Example: C810–Canadian Liter.

811–818	– Specific forms of American Literature
	811 – Poetry
	812 – Drama
	813 – Fiction
	814 – Essays
	815 – Speeches
	816 – Letters
	817 – Satire & Humour
	818 – Misc. Writings
819	– Local emphasis
820	– Anglo–Saxon and <u>English</u> language —
	– Literature of specific countries may be distinguished by using letters.
821–828	– Various forms of English Literature
829	– Old English
830	– German Literature
840	– Romance languages with emphasis of French literature.

841–848	– Various forms of literature (French)
849	– Old French Language
850	– Italian, Romanian and Rhaeto-Romanic language.
860	– Spanish and Portuguese literature
870	– Italic language and Latin
880	– Hellentic language, classical and Greek literature.
890	– Literature of other languages
891	– East-Indo-European languages
892	– Afro-Asiatic languages
893	– Hemitic and Chad languages
894	– Ural-Altaic languages (Turkish, Finnish, Estonian, Paleosiberian languages)
895	– East and South East ASIA (Chinese, Japanese, Korean, Burmese)
896	– African languages
897–898	– American and South American languages
899	– Other languages (Tagalok, Bahasa, Indonesia and Esperanto)

Example:

Biographies of Hindi poets upto 19th century:

891.43	– Hindi
–1	(Table 3) – Poetry
11–19	– Poetry of specific period
1009	– History, description (collection) (Biography of poets of more than one period) (Add No. following 10 in 1001–1009 = [10]09)

= 891.431509.

17

900 – Geography and History

900	– General works on history
901	– Philosophy and theory of general history.
901.9	– Civilisation (General works)
902.3	– Misc. works (chronologies) and dictionary, encyclopedia, concordances.
904	– Specific events of natural origin (Earthquakes). Events of human origin (Battle, fires)
905–908	– Serial publications, organization, study and teaching.
907.2	– Historiography – Collection of general history
909	– World history – Works on ethnic, racial and national group not limited to any area, country or locality.
910	– General geography and travel – Philosophy and theory of geography – Physical geography not limited to any area, country and locality.
910.2–910.99	– Geographer Explorers Travelers

	Discovery and exploration by specific country.
911	– Historical geography
912	– Earth surface and its graphic presentation including: (a) Atlas (b) Maps (c) Charts (d) Plans
913–919	– Geography and travel in specific continents, countries, localities and extra-terrestrial worlds.
913	– Geography and travel of ancient world.
913.031	–
914–919	– Geography and travel in the modern world.
920	– General biography, genealogy, insignia
920.1–928.9	– Biography of specific classes of persons
929	– Genealogy, names, insignia
930–990	– General history of ancient world
	– Auxiliary table of standard subdivision
930	– General history of ancient world upto ca. 499.
930.1	– Archaeology
930.11–930.16	– Specific archaeological ages
931–939	– Specific places
931	– China upto 420 AD
932	– Egypt upto 640 AD
933	– Palestine upto 70 AD
934	– India upto 647 AD
935	– Mesopotamia and Iranian Plateau upto 637 AD.
936	– Europe north and west of Italian peninsula upto ca. 499.

937	– Italian peninsula upto 676 AD
938	– Greece upto 323 AD
939	– Other parts of ancient world upto 640 AD.
940	– General history of Europe (Western Europe).
940.1	– Early history to 1453
.2	– Modern period, 1453
.3	– World War I, 1914-1918
.4	– Military history of World War I (conduct of war).
.5	– 20th century, 1918 –
.53	– World War II, 1939–45.
.54	– Military history of World War II
941	– British Isles
.1	– Scotland
.5	– Ireland
.6	– Northern Ireland, Ulster
.7	– Republic of Ireland (Eire)
942	– England and Wales
943	– Germany
.1	– North Eastern Germany
.6	– Austria
.7	– Czechoslovakia
.8	– Poland
.9	– Hungary
944	– France
945	– Italy
946	– Spain (Iberian Peninsula)
.9	– Portugal
947	– Russia (USSR)
948	– Scandinavia
.1	– Norway
.5	– Sweden
.9	– Denmark and Finland

949	– Other parts of Europe
.2	– Netherland (Holland)
.3	– Belgium
.4	– Switzerland
.5	– Greece
.6	– Balkan peninsula
.7	– Yugoslavia and Bulgaria
.8	– Romania
.9	– Aegean Sea Islands
950	– General history of Asia
.1	– Early history to 1162
.2	– Mongol and Tatar Empire 1162–1480
.3	– European Exploration 1480–1905
.4	– 20th century
951	– China and adjacent areas
.2	– South Eastern China
.9	– Korea
952	– Japan
953	– Arabian peninsula
.8	– Saudi Arabia
954	– South Asia – INDIA
.022	– Muslim conquests 997–1206
.0223	– Ghazni dynasty 997–1196
.0234	– Khilji dynasty 1290–1320
.025	– Mughal empire 1526–1707
.03	– British rule 1785–1947
.031	– East India Co. 1785–1958
.04	– Independence and partition 1947–1971
954.9	– Pakistan
.92	– Bangladesh
955	– Iran (Persia)
956	– Middle East
.1	– Turkey and Cyprus

.7	–	Iraq
.91	–	Syria
.92	–	Lebanon
.94	–	Israil
.95	–	Jordan
957	–	Siberia
958	–	Central Asia
.1	–	Afghanistan
.4	–	Turkistan
.5	–	Turkmenistan Soviet Socialist Republic
.6	–	Tajikistan
.7	–	Uzbekistan
959	–	South East Asia
.1	–	Myanmar
.3	–	Thailand
.4	–	Laos
.5	–	Commonwealth of Nations — Malaysia
.52	–	Singapore
.6	–	Cambodia
.7	–	Vietnam
.8	–	Indonesia
.9	–	Philippines
960	–	AFRICA
961	–	North Africa
.1	–	Tunisia
.2	–	Libya
962	–	Egypt and Sudan
.4	–	SUDAN
963	–	Ethiopia (Abyssinia)
964	–	North West African Coast (Morocco)
965	–	Algeria
966	–	West Africa
.23	–	Mali
.3	–	Senegal
.6	–	Liberia

.68	–	Ivory Coast
.7	–	Ghana
.81	–	Togo
.9	–	Nigeria
967	–	Central Africa
.1	–	Lower Guinea area — Guinea
.24	–	Republic of the Congo
.3	–	Angola
.43	–	Chad
.51	–	Zaire
.61	–	Uganda
.62	–	Kenya
.7	–	Somaliland
.73	–	Somalia
.8	–	Tanzania
.81	–	Zanjibar
.9	–	Mozambique
968	–	South Africa
.7	–	Cape of good hope
.8	–	Namibia
.9	–	Rhodesia, Zambia, Malawi
969	–	South Indian Ocean Island
.1	–	Madagascar
.8	–	Macarena Islands
.82	–	Mauritius
970	–	NORTH AMERICA
971	–	Canada
972	–	Mexico
.8	–	Central America
.81	–	Guatemala
.84	–	El Salvador
.85	–	Nicaragua
.87	–	Panama
.9	–	West Indies

.91	–	Cuba
.92	–	Jamaica
.983	–	Trinidad
973	–	United States
974	–	North Eastern United States
.2	–	New Hampshire
.7	–	New York
.8	–	Pennsylvania
.9	–	New Jersey
975	–	South Eastern United States
.2	–	Maryland
.5	–	Virginia
.8	–	Georgia
.9	–	Florida
976	–	South Central United States
.2	–	Mississippi
.4	–	Texas
.7	–	Arkansas
977	–	North Central United States
.1	–	Ohio
.2	–	Indiana
.3	–	Illinois
.4	–	Michigan
.6	–	Minnesota
.7	–	Iowa
.8	–	Missouri
978	–	Western United States
.1	–	Kansas
.2	–	Nebraska
.3	–	South Dakota
.8	–	Colorado
.9	–	New Mexico
979	–	Pacific Coast States (slope region of USA)

981	– Brazil
982	– Argentina
983	– Chile
984	– Bolivia
985	– Peru
986	– Colombia and Ecuador
.1	– Colombia
.2	– Ecuador
987	– Venezuela
988	– Guyana
989	– Paraguay and Uruguay
990	– Other parts of the world
993.1	– New Zealand
994	– Australia
995	– New Guinea (Papua)
996	– Polynesia
.9	– Hawaii
997	– Atlantic Ocean Island
998	– Arctic Island and Antarctica
999	– Extra-terrestrial worlds

Examples:

1. Historians and historiographers of Western Europe

940	–	European history
.007202	–	Historiography and Historian (Auxiliary).

   = 940.<u>007202</u>

2. Smith, William, New Voyage to Guinea 1967

916	–	Travel in Africa
04	–	Travel (Auxiliary Schedule)
= 6718	–	Guinea
= 916.671804		

3. Important discoveries and an a/c of travel in 5th century

913.04	–	Travel
[0901]5	–	5th century (TI-SSD)
= 913.045		

4. Discoveries by Portuguese

910.93	–	Discoveries
[9]469	–	Portuguese
= 910.90469		

5. Gazetteer of India. India govt. 1965

954	–	India (914–919)
03	–	Dictionary, Ency., concordances
915	–	Geography of Specific countries
= 915.40<u>03</u> (One 0 is to be added in 03).		

6. History and civilization of Greeks upto 15th century

909	–	General World history
.04	–	Ethnic, racial, national group civilization (01–99 from table 5 and add 0 to the result add the number following 909.1–909.8)
–81	–	Ancient Greeks (Table 5)
909.4		(1400–1499)
= 909.64810<u>4</u>		(1400–1499 0 to be added)

7. Civilization of Canadians living in Asia

909	–	Civilization (Direction in 909.9)
.011	–	(Racial, ethnic) Canadian
		032

RULES

Geography, History and Auxiliary disciplines

Main Subjects

1   General geography
2   History
31 General biography
32 Genealogy, names, insignia

Subjects covered under 900

Social situations and conditions
General political history

Military
Diplomatic
Political
Economic
Social Welfare aspects of specific wars
Point of view

900.1–900.9	Standard subdivisions of Geography and History.
910–919	Geography and travel
920–929	Biography, Genealogy, insignia
901.909–939–990	History
1. 900.1–900.9	Standard subdivisions of Geography and History.

As per enumeration in the schedule two zeroes are to be used for standard subdivisions of geography and history when both the subjects are described together in the document.

= Geography + History = Used together
= two zeroes (00) are used.

Example: Serial publications of Geography and History
= 900.5   900 + 05 = 900.5

Organization of geography and history
900 + 06   = 900.6

2. 910–919 Geography and travels —
Main divisions of 910–919

(a) 910.02 Physical geography
(Area, regions and places in general)
02 from special table

Examples:

(1) Physical geography of coastal regions
910.02 + 146

910.02	Physical geography (Add to area notation from T.2 to base No. 910.02)
146	Coastal regions
= 910.2146	

(2) Physical geography of rural regions

> 910.02   Physical geography
> –[1]734   Table 2
> = 910.02734

910.1 Topical geography

Geography related to specific subjects.

Example: Economic geography of India

> 910.1   Topical geography

Add 001–899 to base number 910.1 then add 0 and to the result add notation 1–9 from table 2.

> 330   Economic (001–899)
> –54   India
> = 910.133054 <u>or</u> 330.9

> 330.9   Economic geography
> 355.47   Military geography
> 525   Astronomical geography
> 526   Mathematical geography

3. 910.3 Dictionaries, Gazetteers

General <u>geographical</u> dictionary, concordances, gazetteers and works on place names systematically arranged for ready reference are to be classed in 910.3.

Example:

> (1) Webster geographical dictionary
>   910.3

> (2) Statesman's Yearbook World Gazetteer
>   910.3

4. <u>Travel</u>

The number relating to travel may be grouped into —

• (a) 910   Travel — general treatment
(b) 910–919   Travel in specific continents, countries.....

910 Travel general treatment

There are readymade class numbers under 910, *e.g.*

> 910.202   World travel guide
> 910.4   Accounts of travel
> 910.41   Trips around the world

5. Discovery and Exploration

910.93–.99   By specific countries
913–919   in specific continents, countries
910.9   discoveries and explorations by one specific country in general.

Examples:

(1) Discovery of Portuguese

Base No.   Area No. 1 for country responsible
                              (T.2)
910.9   + –469
= 910.469

(2) Exploration by United States

Base No.   Table 2
910.9   –73
= 910.973

6. Excursions — into unknown or little known areas

913–919

Using 04 from special table under 913–919.

Examples:

(1) Exploration by India of Antarctica

Base No.   Area   Special Table
91   +   –989   +   04
= 919.8904

(2) Exploration by United States of Antarctica in 20th century.

Base No.   T2   Spl. Table   Nos. following 973
91   + –989 +   04   +   [973].9

6.   (a) Initial exploration of a place and early history of the country = 930–990.

Examples:

(1) French explorations in North America 970.018

(2) Spanish discovery and exploration in

Panama, 1901–1515

= 972.8012

911 Historical Geography = 911

Growth and changes in political divisions of specific countries and localities.

It is also used for historical Atlases and maps

Examples:

(1) New political divisions of former USSR

    Base No.   T2

    911   + −47

    = 911.47

(2) Historical map of India

    Base No.   Table 2

    911   + −54

    = 911.54.

912 Graphic Representation of Surface of Earth

It includes graphic representation of surface of earth and extra-terrestrial world in the form of —

1. Maps
2. Atlases
3. Charts
4. Plans

Example:

Maps locating monastic schools of Buddhism

Base No.   Add 001–899

9121   +   377.3

   = 912.13773

912.1   Maps of areas, regions, places in general

Examples:

(1) Maps of Arabian sea

    Base No.   Nos. following −1

    912.19   [−1]6537

    = 912.196537

(2) Maps of specific continents, countries......

Example: Bihar in maps

Base No.	Area T.2
912	–5412
= 912.5412	

913-919 – <u>Geography and travels in</u>

913 – <u>Ancient world</u> – <u>and</u>

914–919 – Specific continents, countries, localities in Modern world <u>and</u> Extra-terrestrial world.

All other directions in schedule should be utilized.

Standard subdivision 001–009 should also be used.

Examples:

(1) City directories and telephone books of Rajasthan

Base No.	Areas T.2	Spl. Table use 001–008 for S.S.
91	+ –544 +	–005
= 915.440025		

(2) Gazetteer of India 4 vols.

Base No.	Area T.2	Spl. Table use 001–008 for SS
91	+ –54	–003
= 915.4003		

Use of other numbers of the special Table 01–09

01–09 are used for following subjects —

01	Prehistorical geography
02	Physical Geography
04	Travel
09	Areas, regions, places in general.

Example:

<u>01</u> Prehistoric geography of China

–31 Ancient China

Base No.	T2	Spl. Table
91	+ –31 +	01
= 913.101		

02 The Earth (Physical geography)

Physical geography of Rajasthan

Base No.		T2		Spl. Table
91	+	–544	+	02

= 915.4402

04 Travel

Narrative of a journey through upper provinces of India from 1824–1828 in 3 vols.

04   Travel

041–049 Historical periods

Add to 04 the historical period numbers following 0 that appear in subdivisions of 930–990

954.0313 1807–1828

Base No.		Area T.2		Spl. Table No.		No. following 0 in 939–990
91	+	–54	+	04		[954.0]313

= 915.404313

09 Areas, regions, places in general

Add to 09 the numbers following–1 in notation 11–18 from table 2.

Example:

Geography of rural regions of India

–1734 Rural regions (T2)

Base No.		Table 2		Spl. Table		Table 2 nos. following –1
91	+	–54	+	09		[–1]734

= 915.409734.

BIOGRAPHY, GENEALOGY, INSIGNIA

Autobiography
Diaries
Reminiscences
Correspondence

920 Biography is divided in two main divisions

1. General collection and biography
2. Individual or collective biographies of persons associated with specific discipline or subject.

1. General Collection of Biography

It is divided into five subdivisions:

(a) General collection of biography by period

It includes the collection of biographies of persons who are associated with various disciplines or subjects or belonging to different areas, but are of a common period.

Such a collection is to be classified under 920.00901 – .00905 Historical periods.

Steps

(i) Write base number 920.0090

(ii) Add numbers following 090 in 'Standard subdivisions' notations 0901–0905 from table 1.

Examples:

(1) Current biography, Monthly 1940

Base No.　　　Add Nos. following –090 from T.1
920.0090　+　　　　[–090]44
= 920.009044.

(2) Who's who — an annual biographical dictionary, 1949, London

Base No.　　　Add Nos. following 090 from T1
920.0090　+　　　　[–090]34
= 920.009034.

(b) 902.0091 Area, region, place in general

General bibliographies not associated with any specific continent, country, or locality.

But associated with general physiographical regions or socio-economic regions or other kinds of terrestrial regions, it is classified under 920.009.

Examples:

(1) Who's who in Afro-Asian bloc

Base No.		Area table 2		
920.009	+	−17165	=	920.00917165

(2) Biographies of eminent living personalities in under-developed countries of the world

Base No.		Area Table		
920.009	+	−1724	=	920.0091724

(c) <u>General collection of biography by continents, countries, localities</u>

A general collection of biography of persons not associated with one specific subject but belong to specific continents, countries or localities, such collection of biography is to be classified under 920.03–.09.

Example:

Dictionary of national biography — 4 Vols.

Base No.		Area T.2
920.0	+	−54
= 920.054.		

(d) <u>General collection of biography by Racial, Ethnic, National group</u>

General collection of biography relating to —

> Racial
> Ethnic group
> National group

–although not to residing in one specific continent, country or locality or not associated with one specific discipline or subject —

> It is to be classified under 920.0092
> + Adding to it notation from Table 5.

Examples:

(1) A collective biography of Indians

Base No.		Table 5
920.0092	+	−91411
= 920.009291411.		

(2) A general collections of biography of Spanish Americans

    Base No.   Table 5

    920.0092   +   −68

    = 920.009268.

(e) <u>General collection of biography NOT limited by period, place, group and NOT associated with specific subjects.</u>

A general bibliography which is

   (i) Not limited by period

  (ii) Not limited by place

 (iii) Not limited by group

<u>Not associated</u> —

  (a) With specific subjects

Example:

    Chambers biographical dictionary = 920.02

    Websters biographical dictionary = 920.02

2. <u>920.1 – 928.9 Individual and collected biography or persons associated with specific discipline or subject</u>

  (i) Specific classes of persons —
    Biography 920.1 – 928.9
    Specific subject + −092 from table of SS

  (ii) Individual biography – 92 or 920.

Examples:

(1) Biography of Dr. S.R. Ranganathan of India

    <u>020</u>.92454   *or*   <u>920</u>.254

    Specific   Biography
    subject   (Individual)

(2) Biography of V.K.R.V. Rao, an Economist of India

    923.3   +   54 (T2)
    = 923.354   or
    330   +   092 (SS)   54 (T2)
    = 330.09254.

(3) Collections of biography of fiction writers in Hindi language

    Base No.   T6
     928   +   –91431
    =928.91431.

(4) Who's who in magic and witchcraft from past to present

    Base No.   Add from 001–999
    920.9   +   133.43
    =920.913343
        or
   133.43092   (using SS notation –92).

(5) Biography of Sunil Gavaskar

    Base No.   Add Nos. following 7
    927   +   [7]96.358
     = 927.96358
       or
    796.358092 (SS–092).

Biography of Historian and Historiographer

    Individual   –   907.202
    Specialising in world history –   907.202
    Specialisation in specific area –   007202
      (from specific table for 930–990)

(1) Biography of an Indian historian who specialises in British history

    Base No.   Notation from Spl. Table under 930–999
    941   +   007202
    = 941.007202.

(2) Biography of an Indian historian who specialises in Victorian period 1837–1901

    941   History of Great Britain
    941.081   Victoria 1837–1901
    –0924   Biography (SS T.1)
     = 941.0810924.

<u>Biography of Discoverers, explorers, travelers</u> = SS notation 092

04 Travel of special class + 092 (SST1)
    (04 from 913–919)

Examples:

(1)   General collections of biography of Indian travelers

Base No.		T.2		Spl.Table		T1
91	+	–54	+	04	+	0922

= 915.4040922.

(2) Biography of Indian travelers   T1

Base No.		T.2	Spl. Table		
91	+	–54	913–919		
			+	04	0924

= 915.4040924.

929 Genealogy, Names, Insignia

Genealogy – Decent families/Geneous families
             Pedigree of a particular person or family.

Insignia   – Sign or mark for identifying the official
             position, honour, status of a country,
             organization, association or individual.

929.1 Genealogy

It is a comprehensive number of works providing information about genealogy.

This number is also used for —

(a) Techniques of compiling family history
(b) Genealogical sources.

929.2 Family history

When family histories are arranged alphabetically by name.
                    Or
Classifying documents relating to family history.

 (a) Family to a specific occupation

Example:

        Tatas family of industrialists = 338.0922.

 (b) Prominent persons of the family

Example:

>   Family history and life of Indira Gandhi
>   = 954.9220924.

(c) Area of the family

Example:

>   Life and history of Nehru family
>   = 929.220954.

(d) Country where family currently lives.

(e) Area in which family lives.

Example

History of prominent families in Bombay city = 954.792

History of a royal family – 929.7 (<u>not</u> 929.2).

929.3 Genealogical sources

>   Records for Genealogical purposes — 929.3

>   Sources —   Wills
>   Text lists
>   Court records
>   Census records

Published by Genealogical agency or by the government.

Example:

Census records of India = 319.14.

Class number 929.3 may be further subdivided by using Areas and historical periods.

Example:

Genealogical sources from 1920–1929
= 929.309042

Genealogical sources from Kashmir
929.3 + –546 = 929.3546

General History

901–908   Standard subdivisions of history
909   World history
930–990   History of specific continents, countries, localities, of extra-terrestrial world.

901–908 Standard Subdivisions History

Standard subdivisions enumerated numbers
+ subdivisions in Table 1.

Example:

Chronological outlines of general history = 902.02

An Index to general history = 901.6

909 World History

909.04		History related to — Racial Ethnic National groups
909.07 – 909.08	–	General history periods
909.1–909.8	–	Specific historical periods
909.09	–	History related to Area, region, places in general.

909.4 Racial, Ethnic, National groups

1. Add notation from table 5 as instructions
2. One provided under 909.4
3. Add 0 as connecting digit (for Area notation)
4. Add number following 909 in 909.1–909.8

Example:

    World history of Indians

Base No.		T.5
909.04	+	–91411
= 909.0491411		

World history of Indians upto 19th century

Base No.	T5		Add		Nos. following 909
909.04	+ 91411	+	00	+	[909.]81
= 909.04914110081					

0 History of Indians in Great Britain

Base No.		T5		Add		T2
909.04	+	91411	+	0	+	41
= 909.0491411041.						

World history – Historical periods

Modern world history   = 909.18
History of 20th century   = 909.82

909.09 General world history of areas, regions, places in general

Areas and Regions are enumerated under

    –1 of table 2 are to be added after 909.09.

Steps

1. Base number 909.09

2. Add to the area notation following –1 from T.2

3. Then add one <u>0</u> as connecting digit if document deals with specific period

4. Then add to this, numbers following 909 in 901.1-909.8

History of Third-World countries

Base No.		T2 Nos following –1
909.09	+	[–1]724
= 909.09724		

History of Third-World countries from 1970–1989

Base No.	T2 Nos. Following –1		Add		Add nos. following 909
909.09	+ [–1]724	+	0	+	[909.]828
= 909.097240828					

    939–990 History of specific continents, countries, localities of extra-terrestrial world

930	– Ancient world
940–990	– Modern world

Example:

934.06   Gupta Dynasty
940.21   History of Europe during renaissance
954.007202 (9 + 52 + 007202) Historians of Japan

History and civilization of the native races of Sikkim

Base No.	T2		Spl. Table		T5
9	+ 54167	+	004	+	011
= 954.167004011					

WAR – 940.54   Military history of War

Intelligence operations of Germany during World War-II
= 940.548743

French unit in World War-I = 940.41244

Personnel narrations of Indian soldiers during World
War-II
= 940.548154

Personal experiences of a librarian of World War-II
= 020.92

<u>Archaeology</u> = Ancient history
= 930.1

Discovery of remains   930.10282

Iron age   930.16

Archaeology of specific places

Instructions under 930–939

3   Ancient world (T2)

940–990   <u>Those places</u> for which numbers are not
available in 3 Ancient world (T2) are to be
classed in 940–990.

Archaeology of Ancient India
= 934.01

Archaeological study of Australia
= 994.01

Archaeology of specific oceans and seas in 909.0963–
909.0967

> *e.g.* Caribbean sea
> Industrial archaeology 609
> Special table
> Special table under 930–990
> Area notation from Table 2

History and civilization of Afro-Americans in Canada

Base No.		Area 3–9		Notation from spl. Table		Notation from T5
9	+	71	+	004	+	–96

= 971.00496.

Indian historians and historiographers

Base No.   Area 3–9 of T2   Notation from spl. Table
 9   +   –54   +   007202
= 954.007202.

Examples:

1. Columbia Lippincatt Gazetteer of the world = 910.3

2. Archaeological remains — interpretation = 930.10285

3. Japan an official guidebook of Japan Travel Bureau = 915.204

4. World travel guide = 910.202

5. Who's who in India = 920.054

6. Royal houses of Netherlands = 929.792

7. Social, political, Economic history of India from 1861–1865 = 973.71.

18

Exercise — Tablewise

Tables 1–30

1. Clock and watch maintenance and repairs = 681.110288
2. Agricultural charts = 630.20122
3. History of South-South countries = 909.09724
4. Noise pollution in Rajasthan = 155.81
5. A bibliography of books on Sikhism = 294.6016
6. Theories of heat transfer = 536.2001
7. Effect of social conditions and fact as on Architecture = 720.103
8. A guide in holy places of India = 263.04243
9. Collection of literature by rural authors = 808.8991734
10. Arabic-Hindi dictionary = 492.7391431
11. Languages of Asia = 409.5
12. Evaluation of sociological Hindi fictions = 891.43308309
13. A Collection of Punjabi language literature by residents of Canada = 891.42080971
14. Dialects of Canada = 427.971
15. Japanese prose literature of late 19th century = 894.68408
16. Chinese language collections = 089.951
17. Migration from Bangladesh to India = 304.85405492
18. A study of National flag = 929.92
19. Social services of homeless people = 362.5

20. Russians in India = 305.89171054
21. Comprehensive biographical dictionary of Bengalis = 920.00929144
22. Cloud seeding = 551.6876
23. Reviews of educational and entertainment films = 028.137
24. Marble mining in Rajasthan = 622.351209544
25. Architectural construction in asbestos = 721.044995
26. Research in Sanskrit rhetorics = 808.04912072
27. Surgery of wounds and injuries of horses = 636.108971
28. Need of environmental protection = 363.7
29. Indian school of economic thought = 330.150954
30. Foreign relations of China with India = 327.54051.

19

Practice

Table 1

1. Classified sales catalogue of

Periodicals	017.4343
Catalogue	017
Classified	017.4 (p. 15)
Periodicals	34 (p. 10)

2. Catalogue of private and family libraries   018.2

Catalogue (author)   018

(Add to base number 018 the numbers following 017 in 017.1–.017.4)

Private and family libraries = [017].2

3. Library building in 1970 in India   022.33054

Library building   022.33

India   054

4. Administration Secondary school libraries   025.1978223

5. Adm. of map collection in a map library   025.176

6. Selection in academic libraries   025.2187

7. Acquisition of material in social sciences   025.273

8. Acquisition of maps   025.286

9. Classification of public administration   025.4235

10. Subject heading in Science   025.495
                                                        ＼
                                                          Asia

11. Orientation in public libraries   025.5674

12. Reviews of works for children and
    young adults   028.162

13. Dutch language encyclopedia   033.931(T2)

14. French language encyclopedia   034.1 (T6)

15. Swedish language serial publications 058.7

16. Bibliography of Decimal
    classification   016.025431

17. Subject heading in Agriculture   025.4963

18. Salaries for librarians   331.28102

19. Job opportunities in library
    profession   331.124102

20. Cooperative milk production   334.371

21. Unemployment in chemical
    industries   331.1378

22. Prices of wheat   338.13311

23. Disease of respiratory system of
    old people   618.97<u>62</u>
                                                      ／
                                             Respiration system

24. Rites and ceremonies in Jainism   294.438

25. Attitude of Buddhism towards crime 294.3317833

26. Sterio Chemistry of Alkaloids   547.7204423
    (from [541.2]<u>23</u>)

27. Power of U.S. President
    (351.00322)   353.0<u>22</u>Power

28. Heart disease specialists   616.1202461

Table 2

29. Elementary education in Tamil
    speaking area in Dacca (Tamil
    from language table p. 427)   372.954922094811

30. North American foreign policy towards non-aligned countries (un-aligned countries) (unaligned block T.2, p. 25)   327.70 <u>1716</u>

31. Treaties between India and Bhutan   341.026665405498

32. Christian religious congregations in China   255.<u>00951</u>

                      /   \

               (p. 135) China

33. Public worship in Roman Catholic Churches in India   264.0200954 (p. 146)

34. Crimes in rural regions of Andhra Pradesh   364.9173405484(T2)

35. School libraries in rural regions in India   027.82540<u>1734(T2)</u>

                      /

               Base number

36. Study of Juvenile delinquents of underdeveloped countries of Asia   364.36095009724

37. Crimes in cities of China   364.91732051

38. Emigration from India to USA   325.19540973

39. Foreign policy of India towards USA   327.54073

40. Trade between India and Western block   382.095401713

41. Trade between India and Australia   382.0954094

42. Trade agreement between India and Australia   382.954094

Table 3

43. History of drama displaying love   809.29354

44. Collection of Telugu literature   894.847<u>08</u>

                     /

              Collection

45. An Anthology of Malyalam lyrical   894.812108354

46. Hindi Tragedy (p. 2 vol. 1)   491.4308016

47. History of American Epic poetry   811.0309 History
    (T. 3, p. 399)

48. Critical appraisal of Victorian fiction 823.8

49. Contribution of Hindi literature by
    Bengalis   891.4309144

50. Earlier 20th century Punjabi fiction 891.4235 20th c.
    |
    fiction

51. Collection of contemporary Tamil
    poetry by Sri Lankan authors   894.8111708091413

        Poetry Contemporary Collection

52. Tagore poetry : critical
    appraisal   891.4415 modern period
    |
    Poetry

Table 4 (Individual languages)

53. Tamil readers for Hindi people   894.8118649143
    (T. 4 p. 407) (T. 5 p. 411)

54. English slang   427.09 (p. 601)

55. Indian English   427.954 (p. 601)

56. Greek-Latin Dictionary 480+3+4+470 483.71 Latin
    |
    Dictionary

57. Sanskrit words in Tamil language   494.81124912
    |
    (p. 405)

58. Punctuation of German language   431.1

    Paintings of flowers by poets
    Painting   650
    Other subjects   658
    Plants   658.5

Flowers	658.42
Poets – T1 = 088	T7 . 81
= 658.4208881	

Table 5

1. World History of Jews	909.04<u>924</u>
2. Dravidian Literature 089.88 + 948	809.88948
3. Social study of Indians 305.8 + 91411	305.891411
4. Education of Tibetians 371.97 + 954	371.97954

Table 2: Areas

1. These are to show division or limitation by places, *i.e.* Geographical subdivision.

   General kinds of geographical subdivision —

   (a) Land forms
   (b) Oceans
   (c) Specific continents
   (d) Countries

2. Any class may need geographical subdivision at some time.

3. In some classes place is one of the important kinds of subdivision.

4. D.C. give specific instructions on what to do.

   Example:

   Historical and Geographical treatment of General Clubs
   General Clubs in Sweden = 367
   (.91 - .99 Geog. Treatment)
   Add Area notation 1-9 to base number 367.9
   If in Sweden = 367.9485

   <u>Wages in France</u>
   Wages – 331.2944
   (Area notation)
   291-299 Geog. Treatment
   (Add area notation 1-9)

5. Some, not all the area tables are relevant for dividing a given class number and the instructions in D.C. may

limit the area notation to be used. This sometimes looks confusing but it is just the same as the method we have seen already.

Example: Public education in India 379.54.

6. There are many numbers in schedule. Where no instruction is given at all.

For instance mining has no special subdivision for historical and geographical treatment, and thus <u>A History of Mining</u> will naturally be 622.09 and since the standard subdivision – 09 contains –093 –099.

Add 'Area' notation 3-9 from table 2 to base number –09.

Example: Silviculture in Greece
634.95<u>09495</u>

Birds of Antarctica – 598.2<u>989</u>
(already provided)

Table 3: Literature Class

Five Steps

Table 3 is a subdivision of individual literatures.

1. At one time DC had many <u>add</u> instructions in this class and you would have had to consult the schedules in general places to find all the pieces of notation that might make up even as apparently simple a subject as <u>Realism in French Classical Drama</u>.

2. Table 3 can be used for 800 class very easily.

3. Table 3 may be used only with class 800 and never with any other.

4. Its notation may be used with a starred number from the schedules — Never alone.

5. The main part of the table is a complete list of features, forms and periods of literature, in various combinations.

6. The last part is a brief indication of how to arrange criticism, biography and the works of single authors.

<u>We are concerned herewith first with parts</u> —

First Parts – Features
　　　　　　　 Forms
　　　　　　　 Period of Literature (in various
　　　　　　　 combinations)

Last Part　 – Arrangement of criticism,
　　　　　　　 Arrangement of Biography,
　　　　　　　 Arrangement of single author.

Example: A collection of Elizabethan English Literature:

English Literature	–	82
Collection (appraisal)	–	0800　(p. 396)
Elizabethan period	–	(p. ＿＿＿)
Class number	–	820.8003

Example: **Modern Tamil Poetry depicting Nationalism**

Tamil Literature –　　　894.811　　＋ 1 ＋ 7　09358

Form (Poetry)　　　　　Base No.　　　　　Notations

　　　　　　　　　　　　　　Poetry　 Modern period

Period of Literature
　　　　Modern – 7

After period — for specific character/feature add the number from Table 3–A after the nation of specific form (1–8 p. 390) with 09 History, critical appraisal.

　　　　　= 09　 358

　　　　(Table 3)　　　Nationally
　　　　p. 390　　　　　Table 3–A
　　　　　　　　　　　　　p. 401

Example: Collection of Tamil poetry depicting idealism

894.811	Tamil Literature
1008	Collection
13	Idealism
= 894.8111008013	

Example: Collected Tamil Literature depicting idealism

894.811	Tamil Literature
08013	Collection

Example: History of 20th century Tamil Literature

894.811	Tamil Literature
09	History (p. 389)
007	20th century (09001-09009)

= 894.81109007

Example: A collection of German language literature by Engineers

German Literature	=	830
Collection	=	080
Historical	=	09262 Engineers
		Persons associated with subject

Rule = 08 – 01 may be divided in 3.

1. Features
2. Elements
3. Themes

Example: English Dramatic Poetry

English Poetry	=	821.02
English Literature	=	82 Base No.
Poetry (Dramatic)	=	102
English Dramatic Poetry	=	821.02

Example: Spanish Drama of the Golden Age

Spanish Literature	=	86
Spanish Drama	=	862
Golden Age	=	862.3

Example: Romanticism in Elizabethan Poetry

English Poetry	=	82 + 1 = 821
Elizabethan period	=	821.3
Romanticism	=	0914 $\ominus$ 821.30914

Example: Plot in 17th century Spanish Novels

Spanish Literature	=	86
Spanish Novels	=	863
17th century	=	3
Plot	=	09 24

Exercise Table 7: Persons

1. Readings for school children

   44   School children
   028.53   Readings by specific age groups
   Add to base number 028.53 the numbers following 05 in 'Persons' notations 054–055 from table 7 = 44 school children.
   = 028.5344

2. Ethics of politician

   Ethics of professionals and occupations
   174.<u>9329</u>
         \
         Politicians

3. Mathematics for Engineers

   510   Maths
   024   Works for specific types of users
   (T.1)   Add 'persons' notations 03–99 from Table 7 to base number –024
   62   (T7)
   = 510.2462

4. Customs of lawyers

   390.4   Customs of peoples of various specific occupations
             Add 'Persons' notations 09–99 from Table 7 to base number 390.4
   34   Persons occupied with Law
   = <u>390</u>. <u>344</u>
      /   \
   Customs   Lawyers

5. Painting of flowers by Poets

   758.42 Paintings of flowers
      088   Treatment among groups of specific kinds of persons
            Add 'persons' notations 04–99 from table 7 to base number –88.

81   With poetry (Persons occupied with creative
            writing and speaking)
= 758.4208881.

Table 6: Exercise

1. <u>English words in Hindi language</u>

   491.43   Hindi language
   –24   Foreign element (T4)
            Add 'Languages' notations 1–9 from table 6
            to –24.

Philosophy 100

1. Ghosts in India   133.12<u>54</u>

2. Medical Astrology   133.58<u>61</u>

   Astrology   – 133.58
   Medical Sc.   – 61

3. Memory   153.12

4. Synesthesia   152.189

5. Test for musical ability   153.94<u>78</u>

6. Psychology of gifted children   155.646345
      155.45
      15 Exceptional children
      [371.9]5 Gifted students

7. Psychology of colour 155.911   155.91145
      Colour [152.1]45

8. Influence of family members   155.924
      155.9
      155.92   Social environment
      [158.2]4   Family members

9. Comparative Reaction time-Studies   157.283
      157.2   Comparative physiological
                 psychology of Animals
      [152.]83   Reaction time studies

10. Comparative learning curves   156.3158
      156.3   Comparative intelligence...animals
      [153].158   Learning curves

11.	Personal improvements	158.1
12.	Oldman of 69	170.20226
13.	Morale of female	170.20244
14.	Ethics of sex and reproduction	176
15.	Critical appraisal of Kent's theory of knowledge	121.09<u>2</u>4
16.	Philosophy of Lebanon	181L
17.	Confusion Philosophy	181.09512
18.	Toist Philosophy	181.09514
19.	Philosophy of Thailand	181.193
20.	Mexican Philosophy	199.72
21.	Psychology of Sumerians	155.849995
22.	Ethics of Librarians	174.9<u>092</u>(T7)
23.	Test of Musical ability	153.9478
24.	Mental Health programme in India	131.32954
25.	Interpretation of dreams	135.3
26.	Psychology of Bengalis	155.849144

200 Religion

1. History of Judaism   296.09
   Judaism   296
   History   09

2. Adventist Secondary Trg. School
   and courses   207.1267
       Secondary Trg. School 207.12
       Adventist Church   [28]<u>6.7</u>

3. Museums, collection on Christianity   207.34
       Education aspects   207.3
       Museums   07<u>4</u>

4. Selection for new testament   225.4

5. Science of Bible   220.85
       Non-religious subject treated in
       Bible   220.8
       Science   <u>5</u>00

6. Individual persons in Bible   225.924
   New Testament   225
   History (Add to base No. 225.9 following
   221.9 in 221.91-221.95)

   Persons individual 221.904

7. Morality discriminatory practices   241.675
   Moral Theology   241
   (Add base number 241.6, the number
   following 17 in 172-179)   675

8. Prayer and meditation for young
   women   242.633
9. Cathedral Church building   246.96
10. Holy family   247.55
11. Conversion of Christians to Judaism   296.71
12. Guides for husbands   248.8425
13. Attitude towards capital punishment   291.1783366
14. Attitude towards pollution   291.1783628
15. Statement on original sin   233.14
16. French missions to Africa   266.2304406
17. Youngmen's Christian Association   267.4
18. Retreats of man   269.642
19. Mahabharat   294.5923
20. Hindu Yogic medication   294.543
21. Mortality of family relationship   294.54863
22. Attitude towards Science   296.3875
23. Importance of moral theology   296.3
24. Attitude of Buddhism towards crime   294.337833
25. Attitude of religions towards women   291.178342
26. Science in Bible   220.85
27. Attributes of God   231.4

300 Social Sciences

1. Psychological effect over population   304.65
2. Migration from United States of America to Australia   304.894073
3. Christian scientist in France   305.685044
4. English speaking people in South Africa   305.721<u>068</u>
5. Chinese in United States   305.89510<u>73</u>
6. Statistics on banking   332.10212
7. Political condition in 13th century   320.9022
8. Political Party of France   324.244
9. Communist Party   324.240975
10. Election of 1964 in India   324.609540904
11. British policies in India   325.31410954
12. Immigrant workers from China to California   325.25109794
13. New York Stock Exchange   332.64273
14. Prices of rice   338.13318
15. Newspaper publishing   338.8261<u>07</u>
16. Collection of treaties on air transport   341.7567<u>07</u>
17. Regulation of industry   343.07
18. Education for blind students   344.079111
19. Contracts of partnership   346.0682
20. Property law of Australia   346.<u>9</u>40<u>4</u>
21. Tax court   343.040<u>269</u>
22. Land Tribunal   346.0430<u>269</u>
23. Judges   346.430269
24. Classification of jobs in labour organization   <u>351</u>.830<u>683</u>
    Labour
    (Personnel
    Mgt. Org.)

25. Use of computer in Govt. accounting 351.72302854

      351.723   1
      0<u>28</u>54 Generalia
      (SS p. 5)

26. Military procurements   355.6212

27. Trade in milk   351.8261<u>71</u> milk

28. Weather forecasting   351.855<u>5163</u>
                      forecasting

29. Agricultural Technology   351.8233 (p. 422)

30. Water pollution   352.942325

31. Nuclear weapons   355.825119

32. Welfare work in 1960-69   361.9<u>046</u> (p. 11)

32. Safety technology in Hydraulic Engg. 627.<u>0289</u> (p. 5)

33. Law as a profession   340.<u>023</u> (p. 4)

34. Education of Jews in France   371.97<u>924</u>0<u>44</u>

35. Education for social responsibility   370.115

36. Educational guidance   378.19422

37. Helicopters   387.73352

38. Customs of lawyers   391.043<u>44</u> (p. 440)

39. Cats among animals   398.2452974422

40. Flowering plants   398.368213

41. Foreign ministry of India   354.54061

42. Rescue operations of flood victims   363.349381(p. 485)

43. Arithmetic curriculum in Elementary
      school   372.72<u>043</u> (p. 530)

44. Audio-Visual methods of teaching
      in Universities   378.1<u>735</u> (p. 519)

45. Trade in Textile   380.14<u>677</u> (p. 552)

46. Costumes of dancers   391.<u>047</u>933 (p. 451)

47. Tamil folk literature upto 1990   398.20<u>494811</u> (T6)

48. Unemployment in library profession   331.1378<u>102</u>

49. Wages in Chemical industries   331.2046

50. Exchange rate between Dollars and Rupees — 332.4560<u>41</u>0<u>54</u>
51. Entertainment tax on cinema — 336.278792
52. U.S. Foreign aid to India — 331.91073054
53. Indian criminal law procedure — 345.050954
54. Encyclopedia of social sciences — 300.3
55. Foreign policy of Italy towards France — 327.45044
56. Economic condition of India — 330.954
57. Television broadcasting by Satellite — 384.55456
58. Administration of Police Department — 350
59. Public education for rural people — 379.272 (p.209)
60. Serials of social welfare work — 361.005
61. Cooperative milk production — 334.<u>374</u> (634.4)
62. River transportation of passengers — 386.3<u>52</u> (572)
63. Facilities of commercial aircraft — 387.73
64. Library Science Student organization — 371.8302
65. Women workers in India — 331.40954
66. Crime in rural region of Rajasthan — 364.<u>917340544</u>
67. Crime in the cities of India — 364.91732054
68. Treaties between India and U.K. — 341.026654042
69. Foreign policy of India towards USA — 327.1154072
70. Trade agreement between France and Australia — 382.944094
71. Research on criminal law of India — 345.0014 (p.1)
72. Teaching of labour laws in Indian Universities — 344.01<u>0711</u>

400 Language

1. Language of India — 409.54
2. Dutch language — 439.31
3. Dialects of London — 427.1
4. Dialects of Bavaria — 437.3

5. Yiddish   437.947

6. Dialects of Southern France   447.8

7. Hittite as a language   491.998

8. Mongolian   494.2

9. Tamil readers of Hindi speaking
people   494.811<u>864</u> <u>91431</u>
             (T4)   (T6)

10. Hindi readers of Tamil speaking
people   491.43<u>864</u> <u>94811</u>

11. Bilingualism in India   404.20954

12. English-Russian Dictionary   423.<u>917</u>/491.7321

13. Turkish   494.<u>35</u> (T6)

14. Rajasthan language   491.479

15. English-Hindi Dictionary   423.91431 (T6)

A. **Russian French Dictionary**

    491.7   Russian
    .3   Dictionary
    −32-39   Bilingual
    −41   French
    = 491.7341

B. Webster's New Dictionary of synonyms, Springfield Massachusetts

    420   English
    −3   Dictionary
    −31   Specialised
    = 423.1

500 Pure Sciences

1. Expansion of functions 515.82

    515.82 Generalia
    34   ([515.2]34) Expansion of functions

2. Jewish calendar —

    529.32   Ancient and Non
               Christian calendar
    [29]6   Judaism (Jewish)
    = 529.326

3. Electron Microscopy — 502.825
4. Arithmetics approximation — 513.24
5. Expansion of functions — 515.82<u>34</u> (p. 627)
6. Ultraviolet radiation — 523.015<u>014</u> (p. 663)
7. Cosmic rays — 523.0197<u>223</u> (p. 675)
8. Cavatation — 533.29
9. Solid State Chemistry — 541.042<u>1</u> (p. 653)
10. Microwave analysis — 544.62 (p. 687)
11. Boric Acid — 546.<u>671</u> <u>22</u> (Ext. schedule)
12. Carboxylic Acids — 547.4<u>37</u> (p. 698)
13. Nylon — 547.85<u>73</u> ([677].73)
14. Marine sediments of Mediterranean Sea — 551.460831<u>638</u> (T2)
15. Red Sea — 551.46716<u>533</u> (T2)
16. Temperature of Indian Ocean — 551.5246<u>5</u>(T2 p. 22)
17. Cloud seeding — 551.68<u>76</u> (p. 721)
18. Gravitational force — 574.19192 (p. 749)
19. Desert biology — 574.909154 (p.16)
20. Astro-biology — 574.99<u>9</u> (T2)
21. Fresh water microorganisms — 576.1929
22. Pathological anatomy of roots — 581.22<u>98</u> (p. 767)
23. Desert plants — 581.90954
24. Ecology — 582.1605 (p. 768)
25. Circulatory fluids — 591.1113 (p. 747)
26. Desert insects — 595.7090954 (T1)
27. Forest birds — 598.291<u>52</u> (T1)
28. Mineralogy of India — 549.9<u>54</u>
29. Rainfall in India — 551.57810954
30. Botanical Gardens of India — 580.74454
31. Encyclopedia of Science and Technology — 503 / 03.5

32. Statistics for teachers — 519.5<u>024377</u> (T7)
33. Orbit of Venus — 523.42 (T1)
34. Velocity and aerodynamics — 533.6227 (p. 662)
35. Molecular structure of Uranium — 546.431<u>42</u> (p. 679)

600 Technology

1. Engineering for arctic regions — 620.4<u>113</u> (p.15)
2. Amplifier — 621.381325
3. Television set — 621.38836
4. Petroleum — 622.18282
5. Components of Jet planes — 629.134/623.746044
6. Design in steel — 669.1420222/623.81821 (T1)
7. Design in plastic — 624.18923
8. Sources of water — 628.11
9. Models of racing cars — 629.221<u>8</u> (p. 1021)
10. Agriculture charts — 630.201<u>22</u> (T1)
11. Palm trees — 634.97<u>45</u> [58]4.5
12. Duck egg — 637.597
13. Public welfare agency — 659.293<u>616</u> (361.6)
14. Pottery dictionary — 666.3<u>3</u>
15. Aluminium — 659.95722
16. Cotton Ginning — 677.2121
17. Body restoration of home — 684.10442
18. Playing cards — 688.7<u>54</u> (p. 1369)
19. Indian Directory of Food technology — 664.<u>002554</u>
20. Textile design — 677.022
21. Cotton weaving — 677.21<u>42</u> (p. 1188)
22. Dictionary of Engineering — 620.<u>003</u>
23. Agricultural Chemistry — 630.2<u>4</u>
24. Dairy farming in India — 637.0954

25. Agricultural irrigation in
    India   631.70954
26. A cookbook on Mexican
    cooking   641.59<u>72</u>
27. Periodicals on cultivating
    and harvesting   631.505

700 Arts

1. Lawyers as artists   704.344 (T7)
2. Arts of Ist century B.C.   709.<u>014</u> (T1)
3. Tokyo Architects   722.12<u>35</u>
4. Buddhist Monasteries   726.78<u>43</u> (p. 178)
5. Public library building   727.824
6. Sculpture in Andhra Pradesh   730.44<u>84</u> (T2)
7. Gold Smithing in 18th century   739.227<u>24</u> (T1)
8. Post cards   741.683
9. Decoration of hotels   747.885 (p. 1252)
10. Epic painting   753.74
11. Paper money in 19th century   769.559034
12. Postage stamp of birds of the
    world   769.564<u>32</u> (p. 1227)
13. Motion picture photography
    of birds   778.538<u>598</u> (p. 812)
14. Photography of Children   779.25 (p. 1226)
15. Folk songs of 17th century   784.40<u>32</u> (T1)
16. Piano playing (Training)   786.30<u>41</u> (786.2<u>1</u>)
17. Stamp collecting   769.56
18. Influence of Radio   791.44<u>013</u> (p. 1363)
19. Country Maches   796.35863
20. Architecture of Hindu Temple   726.<u>145</u> (Religion)
21. Stage treatment of comedy
    of love   792.<u>0909</u> <u>354</u>

    (p. 1364) (T3A)

800 Literature

1. Technical writings in Spanish   808.0666061
2. Collection of love story   808.83<u>85</u> (T3)
3. African Literature   809.88<u>96</u> (T5)
4. 20th century drama in English by   828.99<u>3322</u>(T1)
   New Zealand authors

                                       (p. 1399) (p. 1407)
5. Rhetorics in Tamil Literature   808.04<u>94811</u>(T6)
6. Ancient Tamil poetry : Critical
   study   894.8111109
7. Biography of Sanskrit poets   891.<u>21009</u> (T3)
8. Collection of Hindi literature by   891.43<u>08</u> <u>91</u>71
   Russian author   (T3)   (T5)
9. Research in literary criticism in
   India   801.95<u>072</u>054 (T1)
10. Collection of cartoon fiction   808.836 (T3)
11. English language literature of
    Israel   828.99<u>5694</u> (T1)
12. Collection of historical plays   808.8<u>24</u> (T3 p. 393)

900 Geography and History

1. Civilization of Canadian lives in Asia

        910.03   –   Man and civilization
        2   –   Anglo-Saxon (T5)
        032   –   Anglo-Saxons
        11   –   Canadians (T5)
    = 910.030311105

2. Civilization of Arabs

        910.03   –   Man and civilization
        927   –   Arabs and matters
    = 910.03927   (T5)

3. Civilization of Tibetans

        910.03   –   Tibetans (T5)
        954
    = 910.03954

4. Middle age European civilization

914	–	Europe
03	–	Man and civilization
0.1	–	Early history 476 = 1453 (p. 1458)

= 914.031

5. Civilization of France

914	–	Geography & History
.44	–	France
.03	–	Civilization

= 914.403

6. History of ancient Greek civilization

913	–	Geog. & Travel of Ancient area
.3	–	Area, notation 3 from T.2 Ancient World
–38	–	Greece
03	–	Civilization

= 913.3803

7. Agricultural civilization of 13th century

901.9	–	General history (Theory & Philosophy)
[090]22	–	13th century

= 901.922

8. Physical geography of pacific region

910.2	–	General Geography and History
.9	–	History and civilization
1823	–	Pacific region (T2)

= 910.021823

9. Physical geography of Australia

91[0]	–	Geography
910.[9]	–	Base Number (T2)
02	–	Physical geography

= 910.0298

10. Maps of Northern Hemispheres

912.19 812 Hemispheres

Maps Area

11. Maps locating desert area

        912   –   Maps
        .19   –   Area
        154   –   Desert (T2)
= 912.19154

12. India in Maps, New Delhi, 1951

        912   –   Maps
        .54   –   India
= 912.54

13. Bihar in Maps, 1954

        912   –   Maps
        5412 –   Bihar
= 912.5412

14. Japan, a official guide

        910   –   Geography and history
        91+54 –   Japan
        0202 –   Guide
= 915.200202

15. A collection biography of Indians

        .920   –   Gen. Biography
        0092 –   Ethnic group (T5)
        1411 –   Indian
= 920.009291411

16. Who's who in Western Hemisphere

     920.00911812
     Biography

17. A Gen. Collection of biography of Spanish Americans

        920   –   General biography
        0092 –   of groups
        68   –   Spanish Americans (T2)
= 920.009268

18. Baker's Biographical dictionary of Musicians, N.Y., 1965

        927   – Persons of Arts and recreation
        [7]80.92 – Musicians
= 927.8092
     or – 780.920922

19. The Peerage of France

    929.9   – Royal houses, Peerage
    44   – France
  = 929.744

20. Genealogical sources of Jaipur State

    929.3   – Genealogical
    544   – Rajasthan
  = 929.3544

21. Royal houses of Japan

    929.7999 – Royal houses of countries outside Europe
    52   – Japan
  = 929.799952

22. Economics geography of British Isles

    910.1   – Geography
    33[0]   – Economics
    041   – Britain
  = 910.133041

23. General biography of 19th century

    920.09   – Biography of countries
    009034 – 19th century
  = 920.09009034

24. Basketball player

    927   – Persons in recreation
    96327   – Basketball

25. Refugee people
    940.3159

26. Life in United States Navy
    940.483

27. Air bases in England
    940.544_42_

28. English civil war
    942._62_ (Time of Charles I, 1625–1660)

29. Reign of Terror
    944.044

30. Period of World War II
    940.53 (1939–1945) / 949.71022

31. Mohd. Ayub Khan
    954.91045

32. USSR in later 20th century
    947.0853 / 958.7085

33. Indian in Arizona
    947.<u>491</u> Arizona (p. 1563)
        (p. 153)

34. Colonial period of Guatemala (1535–1821)
    972.8103

35. British period of USA
    976.203

36. Indian in Brazil
    980.4<u>1</u> (T2 81–89)

37. History of World (Europe)
    909.4

38. Map of India
    912.54

39. Gen. Biographical dictionary
    920.003

40. Biography of Melvil Dewey
    020.92

41. India under Indira Gandhi
    954.051

42. History of Ancient Greek civilization
    913.3803

43. Archaeological Survey of India
    915.403

44. Political map of Pakistan
    911.549

45. A collection biography of Indians
    920.009291<u>1411</u>

Other Examples:

Labour Unions	331.8
Labour management	331.89
Strikes	331.892
Strikes among Engineers in Specific industries	331.89282
Other Therapy	615.85
Mental Therapy	615.851
Occupational and Recreational Therapy	615.8515
Religious Therapy	615.852
Land Economics	333
Public control on land	331.1
Individual control on land	333.3

<u>**Tobacco Agriculture**</u> – 633.71

1. History of teaching in Engineering —

   Engineering   620
   .005 – .008   Standard subdivisions
   Notation from Table 1
   = 007   Teaching = 620.007009

2. Study and teaching of Public health —

   Public health   –   614
   Teaching   –   07
   = 614.07

3. Theory of Buddhism —

   Buddhism   –   294.3
   Theory   –   01
   = 294.301

4. Demographic statistics of Punjabis

   Statistics   –   312
   Standard subdivision   –   089
   Treatment among specific races (T5)

5. Rail-road transportation during 1980-85
   Rail road transportation – 385
   (Page 11) 09048 (1980 – 85)
   = 385.09048

6. Dictionary of cats
   Cats   – 636.8
   Dictionary   – 03
   = 636.803

7. Journal of Public Administration
   Public Administration   – 350
   (p. 394) .0001–.996   Standard subdivision = 0005
   = 350.0005

8. History of Economic thought —
   Economic Theory   – 330.1
   History   – 09
   = 330.109

9. Study of Steam locomotives
   Steam Locomotives   – 625.261
   Study and teaching – 07
   = 625.26107

10. Soil and land use survey manual
    Soil land use survey   – 631.47
    Manual   – 0202 (SS T1)   (Page 3)
    = 631.47-0202

11. Dictionary of Library Science terms
    Library Science   – 020
    Dictionary (terms) – 03
    = 02[0].03 = 020.3

12. Research in stage lighting
    Stage lighting   – 792.025
    Research (T1)   – 072
    = 792.025072

13. German-English dictionary of Physics
    Physics   – 530
    Dictionary – 003

Dictionary of Physics   –   530.0331
German (Language)   –   31 (T6)

14. Directory of special libraries

Special libraries   –   026
Directories   –   00025
= 026.00025

15. Handbook of bacteriology

Bacteriology   –   589.9
Bacteriology   –   00202
= 589.900202 (T1)

16. Index of plant breeding

Plant breeding   –   631.53
Index   –   (SS T1)
= 631.53.016

17. Bibliography of Orthopedic surgery

Orthopedic Surgery   –   617.3
Bibliography   –   0016 (T1)
= 617.30016

18. History of Public administration

Public administration   –   350
History   –   0009
= 350.0009

19. Award in Medicine

Medicine   –   610
Awards   –   079
= 61[0].079   = 610.79

20. Statistics of Income Tax

Income Tax   –   336.24
Statistics   –   028
= 336.24028
Or   = 336.240202

21. Outlines of Human anatomy

Human anatomy   –   611
Outline   –   00202
= 611.00202

22. <u>Teaching of Lib. Sc. through correspondence course</u>

    Lib. Sc.   – 020
    Teaching   – 07
    Correspondence course – 07154
    = 020.7154

23. <u>Formulas of Chemistry</u>

    Chemistry   – 540
    Formula   – 0212
    = 540.212

24. <u>Science Museum</u>

    Science   – 500
    Museum   – 074
    = 500.74

25. <u>Unemployment in 20th century</u>

    Unemployment   – 331.137
    20th century   – 0904 (If in schedule
                             direction delete 9)

    = 331.137904

26. <u>History of Public libraries in 19th century</u>

    Public libraries   – 027.4
    History of 19th century – 09034
    = 027.40934

27. <u>Scientific Principles of library management</u>

    Library management   – 020.6
    Scientific principles   – 015
    = 020.6015

28. <u>Classification of Modern Indian languages</u>

    Modern Indian language – 491.4
    Classification   – 012
    = 491.4012

29. <u>Textile technology in 20th century</u>

    Textile Technology   – 677
    20th century   – 0904
    = 677.00904 (as per schedule)

30. Journal of Local Self-Govt.

    Local Self-Govt.   – 352
    Journal (Serial Pub.)   – .0005
    = 352.0005

31. Quarterly journal of physiology of endocrine glands
(Secretion and related functions)

    Physiology   – 612.4
    Journal   – 005
    = 612.4005

32. Research in tuberculosis

    Tuberculosis   – 616.995
    Research   – 0072 (specific subdivision
    = 616.9950072   in 616.1–616.9 specific
        division page 868)

33. Encyclopedia of Yoga

    Yoga   – 613.7046
    Encyclopedia   – 03
    = 613.704603

34. Agricultural Statistics

    Agriculture   – 630.201 (Instructions –
    Statistics   – [0.2]12 Base No. 630.201
    = 630.20112   number following
        02 in SS 021-022 from
        Table 1.
        SS – 0212 statistics)

35. Yearbook of United Nations

    UN   – 341.23
    Yearbook (serial)   – 05
    = 341.2305

36. Television Engineering — a quarterly journal

    Television   – 321388
    Journal   – 005
    = 321.388005

37. <u>Bibliography of Plastic Surgery</u>

    Plastic Surgery   – 617.95
    Bibliography   – <u>0</u>016 (Base 894 = .003–
                               .008 standard
    = 617.950016   subdivision of surgery)

38. <u>Diesel Engine Manual</u>

    Diesel Engine   – 621.436
    Manual   – 0202
    = 621.4360202

39. <u>Trade catalogue of detergent soaps</u>

    Detergent soaps   – 668.14
    Trade catalogue   – 0294   (T1)
    = 668.140294

40. <u>Case study of unmarried mothers</u>

    Unmarried mothers   – 305.8
    Case study   – 0722   (T1)
    = 305.80722

41. <u>Scholarships in higher education in Indian Universities</u>

    Higher education in
    India   – 378.54 (.4–.9)
    Scholarship   – 079
    = 378.54079

42. <u>Theory of Oriental philosophy</u>

    Oriental philosophy – 181 (.001–.008 standard
    Theory   – 001   subdivision T1)
    = 181.001

43. <u>Engineering Colleges</u>

    Engineering   – 620
    College   – <u>0</u>0711
    = 620.00711

44. <u>Doctors and religion</u>

    200.<u>88</u> (T1) Add persons notation 04-99 T7
    Doctors 61 = 200.8861

45. Social law of Australian native races

Social law	– 344
Special ethnic races	– 0089
(T5) Australian	– 9915

= 344.00899915

46. History of high school songs

Songs	– 784.623
(p. 1335) History	– 009

= 784.623009

47. History of foreign policy of United Kingdom

Foreign Policy	– 327
U.K.	– 41
History	– 009

= 327.41009

48. Legal language and Communication

Legal language	– 34[0]
Communication	– 014

= 340.14

49. Science and Art of Indexing

Subject indexing	– 025.48
Philosophy	– 01

= 025.4801

50. Use of abbreviations in legal communication

Legal Law	– 340
Communication	
Abbreviations	– 0148 (T1)

= 340.148

51. Drug abuse among young adults

Drug addition	– 362.293
Treatment among group of specific kinds of persons	– 088 (from T7)
Young adults	– 056 (T7)

= 362.293088056

52. <u>Handicrafts among Nepalis living in India</u>

    Handicrafts   – 745.5089
    Nepalis   – 91495
    India   – <u>0</u> 54
    = 745.508991495054

53. <u>20th century history of people who study birds</u>

    History of Aves (Birds) – 598.09
    20th century   – 04
    = 598.0904

54. <u>Marketing management for manufacturing</u>

    Manufacturing   – 67[0]
    Marketing Management – 0688
    = 670.688

55. <u>Financial Management of Hotels</u>

    Hotels   – 647.94 (p. 1100)
    Financial Management – 0681
    = 647.940681

56. <u>Management of a Book store</u>

    Book store   – 381.45
    Miscellany   – 02
    Management   – 068
    = 068 = 381.4502068

57. <u>Management of Plant for Commercial bank</u>

    Commercial Bank   – 332.12
    Plant Management   – 0682   (T1)
    = 332.120682

58. <u>Personal Management in Factories</u>

    Factory   – 670
    Personal Management – 0683   (T1)
    = 67[0] + 0683
    = 670.683

59. <u>Management of Farm production</u>

    Farm production   – 630
    Production Management– 0685   (T1)
    = 63[0] + 0685 = 630.685

60. <u>Materials Management for Airlines</u>

    Airlines   – 387
    Material Management   – 0687   (T1)
    = 387.0687

61. <u>Work on Trademark in Technology field</u>

    Technology   – 600
    Trademark   – 0275   (T1)
    = 602.75 = 600.275

62. <u>Life Insurance rates for middle aged people</u>

    Life Insurance   – 368.32
    SS – 088
    Old age people   – 0564 = 332.380880564

63. <u>Manual of historical research in social sciences</u>

    Social Science   – 300
    Historical Research   – 0722   (T1)
    = 30[0] + 0722 = 300.722

64. <u>Illustrations of the technique used in Analytical Chemistry</u>

    Analytical Chemistry   – 543
    Technical methods   – 028   (T1)
    = 543.0028

65. <u>Catalogue of documents written by rural authors</u>

    Catalogue   – 013.9
    = 013.91

66. <u>Selected bibliography of bird diseases</u> – 016.59822/ 598.22016

    Subject bibliography   – 016
    Bird diseases   – 598.22
    = 016.598.22   OR   598.22016

67. <u>Directories of special libraries in India</u>

    (Page 30/026)
    Use 026-0001-0260009
    Special libraries   – 026
    Directories   – 0002554
    = 026.0002554

68. <u>Ethics of academicians</u>   – 174.90901
    Ethics   – 174.9
    Academicians   – 0901 (T7)

69. <u>Mythological interpretation of Koran</u> 297.12268
    Koran   – 297.1220
    (27.1221–297.1228 for principles) Interpretation–
    297.1226
    Mythology – [220.6]8 = 8 (Add to base number
    = 297.12268   297.1226 following
                                 in 220.601–220.68)

70. <u>Practical guide to parent-child relationship among</u>
    64678089914
    Family living   – 646.78
  (Parent-child relationship) – 089 (go to T5) (p. 412)
    South Asians   – 914
    = 646.78089914

71. <u>Relation of Indian Govt. with</u> — Punjabis 323.119142054
    Relation with state to its
    residents   – 323.11   (T5–2–9)
    Punjabis   – 9142
    India   – 054
    = 323.119142054

72. <u>Trade relations between India & European communist</u>
    <u>countries</u>
  Commercial relations – 382.3   382.09540171704

73. <u>Standardisation of Weights and Measures</u> 350.821

74. <u>Observation of Atmosphere with Radar</u> 551.6353

75. <u>Physiology of frogs</u>   597.804102
                        (592-599)
    Frog   – 597.89   (04–Add to 04
                           the number following
                           591 in 591.1 – 591.8)
    Physiology   – 1042
    = 597.891042

76. Urinalysis of pestilential cholera 616.93207566

Pestilential cholera	– 616.932 (Add as instructed under 616.1-616.9)
Phythology	– 07 (Add to 07 the numbers following 616.07 in urinalysis)

= 0.7566

77. Hindu limitations of cooking 641.56745
    (29-292-299)

78. Equipment of football game 688.7633 or 796.3344028

Equipment of outdoor games	– 688.76 (Add to base number 688.76
Football [796].333 (Rugby)	number 688.76 the number following 796 in 796.1–796.9)

= [796].333

79. Violin show in Kerala 787.107395483

Violin	– 787.1
Show	– 073
Kerala	– 95483

= 787.107395483

80. Collection of 19th century poetry 808.81034

Collection of poetry –808	(Add to base No. 808.800 the number following 090 in SS notation 0901–0905 T1 = [090]34)

= 808.8034

81. Romanticism in later 20th century Hindu drama 891.4327091[45]

20th century Hindi drama – 891.4327091
                          Drama – 1940 (1422)

82. <u>Physical geography of mountains</u> 910.021430

    Physical geography   – 910.0210<u>9143</u>
                      (p. 1438) Mountain (T2)

83. <u>Teaching of Antarctica history in Indian Universities</u>
                          998.90071<u>854</u>

    Arctic Island   – 998.<u>9</u> 0 <u>07</u> <u>11</u> <u>54</u>

              History   Teaching Universities India

84. <u>Notable American women, 1707–1950 : A biographical dictionary</u> 920.720923

    Biography   – 920.<u>72</u> (p. 1945)
    America   – 0973 = 920720973

85. <u>History of tricolour – The National flag of India</u> 929.920.954

    Flags – 929.92
    India – 0954
    = 929.920954

86. <u>Bead work on table cloth</u> 746.96

    Bead embroidery   – 746.5<u>049</u> <u>6</u>
                              Special subdivision

87. <u>Protection for insect pests in garden crops</u> 635.0427

    Garden crops   – 635
    Generalities   – 04<u>27</u>
    = 635.0427

88. <u>Child care of foster adolescent girls</u> 649.145

    Adolescent girls   649.145
    (1 Homecare of child)

89. <u>Photo duplication techniques for librarians</u> 686.4024092

    Photo duplication – 686.402
    Personnel – 0249 (023.2 – 023.4 paintings)
    Librarian – 092 (T7)

90. <u>Hindi paintings</u> 755.945

91. <u>Design of Tom-Tom instruments</u> 789.12

Index